SLAVERY IN THE UNITED STATES.

BY THE SAME AUTHOR.

I.

Price Five Shillings, Second Edition.

CRIMINAL JURISPRUDENCE,
CONSIDERED IN RELATION TO CEREBRAL ORGANIZATION.

OPINIONS OF THE PRESS.

" Our opinion of its merits was indicated by the space originally devoted to it in our pages, and its value is increased by the way in which the author has cited many events of the past two years as additional corroborations of his theory."—*Spectator.*

" The work is distinguished by a style worthy of its subject; it is clearly, calmly, and classically written, and altogether is worthy the attention of the lawyer, the physician, the philosopher, and the philanthropist."—*Scotsman.*

" Characterised by a high tone of philanthropy, and by a calm, clear, and conclusive method of logical treatment. Harmonizing, as the general purport of this masterly essay does, with views so long and fervidly urged in these columns, we cannot but recommend it to a still more general circulation than it has already so worthily attained."—*Morning Herald.*

" We beg such of our readers as are interested in improving our criminal law, to direct their attention to the evidence of Mr. Sampson."—*Athenæum.*

" A remarkable work. It would be affectation to conceal that the verdict in the case of M'Naughten goes very far to establish the doctrine of Mr. Sampson."—*Fraser.*

"We recommend this work to our readers with an assurance that they will find in it much food for reflection."—*Dr. James Johnson's Medico-Chirurgical Review.*

" We recommend the entire publication to all our readers; not one of whom can rise from a perusal of it without being pleased and instructed, and on the main practical points, we hope, deeply persuaded."—*Monthly Review.*

" One of the most able works which have been written in recent times on criminal jurisprudence viewed in its relation to cerebral organization; and to the merits, sound judgment, and humanity of which, we have already borne our testimony."—*Literary Gazette.*

" We recommend it to general attention."—*Chamber's Edinburgh Journal.*

" The disquisitions of this author are not less interesting than important."—*Liverpool Albion.*

" We heartily recommend this work."—*Legal Observer.*

" Mr. Sampson treats of the abolition of the punishment of death—we have seldom seen a point better argued."—*Justice of the Peace and County Law Recorder.*

" A very acutely written work. For the reception of such a theory the public mind does not appear to be fully prepared, but at the same time it is obvious that the current of opinion is running in that direction. We do not indeed regret altogether the growing disposition to view great crimes as impossible, except to minds of an insane character; for in our opinion it will be a great improvement in criminal legislation, to take obedience to the laws in general as the standard of moral sanity."—*The Jurist.*

" That Mr. Sampson well deserves the success he has enjoyed, nobody will dispute who reads any half-dozen pages of his volume. Statesmen and philanthropists, humanity and Christianity, owe to him a debt of gratitude, for having placed the questions of capital punishment and the insanity of criminals upon intelligible principles, which, if adopted, will put an end to the doubts and difficulties in which these topics have been hitherto involved, and will prepare the way for some rational and satisfactory legislation."—*Law Times.*

" All who are interested—and who is not?—should get Mr. Sampson's work."—*Tyne Pilot.*

" Mr. Sampson supports his Christian purpose by arguments and illustrations that appeal strongly to the reason of the reader. The work is humane, intelligent, and vigorous. It should be extensively circulated. Opposed to the moral of the present law, it nowhere excites resistance to the strength of present institutions. Mild in its principles, it is also gentle in its prompting. What the author sees right to do he would also teach to be rightly done. Mr. Sampson has written well, and there can be none who read his work but will wish well to his theory."—*Monthly Magazine.*

" We welcome Mr. Sampson as a most valuable accession to the band of phrenological advocates of sound criminal jurisprudence."—*Phrenological Journal.*

II.

Price Sixpence.

THE PHRENOLOGICAL THEORY
OF THE
TREATMENT OF CRIMINALS DEFENDED.

In a Letter to JOHN FORBES, Esq., M.D., F.R.S., &c. Editor of the British and Foreign Medical Review.

" The basis of the theory being sound, Dr. Forbes' sophisms will be of little avail against it."—*Literary Gazette.*

" Mr. Sampson's reply is in terms as mild as it is powerful. Its severity consists in its total demolition of his opponents' reasoning."—*Phrenological Journal.*

SLAVERY IN THE UNITED STATES.

A LETTER

TO

THE HON. DANIEL WEBSTER.

By M. B. SAMPSON.

LONDON:
S. HIGHLEY, 32, FLEET STREET.
1845.

LONDON:
Printed by S. & J. BENTLEY, WILSON, and FLEY,
Bangor House, Shoe Lane.

PREFACE

TO THE ENGLISH EDITION.

The following letter has appeared at a time when the people of the United States are too deeply absorbed in the Texan question to give heed to a plan of Abolition. The prospect of annexation has aroused the Planter from depression and intoxicated him with the idea that, by a bold effort, Slavery may not only be upheld but extended, while the friends of freedom,—still, unhappily, a minority in the Republic,—scared by the sudden energy of their opponents, so far from hoping the immediate overthrow of the iniquity would now be well satisfied with the certainty even of preventing its propagation.

But this panic will soon subside, and whichever way the annexation question may be settled, it cannot fail to give increased intensity to Anti-Slavery agitation.

From signs exhibited at the recent Presidential election there is reason to hope that the result of the contest in 1848 may entirely turn upon the views of the candidates regarding Slavery. Every argument in favour of the institution has now become obsolete wherever civilization is known, and the only security for its continued existence is in the apathy of mankind. A question like that of Texan annexation, by dispelling all apathy on the subject, must hasten its approaching doom.

But although this doom cannot be long deferred, there is reason to believe that it will not be wrought out by violence or spoliation. The growing intelligence which has extinguished everything like sympathy with the Slave-holder, has at the same time developed broader views of the economical duties connected with emancipation; so that no measure of reckless legislation is likely now to be attempted.

Whatever, therefore, may be the immediate reception of the plan submitted to the American people in the following letter, the confidence of its Author will in no degree be shaken with regard to its ultimate adoption.

March, 1845.

CONTENTS.

SECTION I.

OF THE INTERESTS INVOLVED IN THE ABOLITION OF SLAVERY, AND THE EXTENT TO WHICH THEY SHOULD BE REGARDED ... 3

SECTION II.

OF THE MEASURES HITHERTO TAKEN FOR THE ABOLITION OF SLAVERY 20

SECTION III.

OF THE MEANS BY WHICH EMANCIPATION SHOULD BE EFFECTED 63

NOTE.

THE RIGHT OF PETITION 87

TO

THE HON. DANIEL WEBSTER.

Sir,

Amidst all that has been written and spoken on the question of Slavery in America, I have never met with any argument in which the claims of each interest seemed to be fairly comprehended. Such statements, however, may have been put forth, although I have not had the fortune to meet with them; and I should therefore abstain from entering upon the subject, but for the belief that in analyzing these claims I shall be able to suggest a plan by which they may be adjusted.

Looking at the question as one of primary importance not only to America but to the world, I cannot address this letter more appropriately than to yourself. Intended only to promote the practical and immediate welfare of all the interests to which it refers, it might be submitted indifferently to a representative of Northern or Southern views. It is because, without reference to those views, you are regarded both at home and abroad with a respect which, in every mind, will survive all differences of the hour, that I seek to gain a patient hearing by the influence of your name.

For the sake of convenience, my remarks will be divided into three sections. First, I propose to consider the various interests involved in the Abolition of Slavery, and the extent to which these interests should be regarded. Next, to point out the evils which must follow any scheme of emancipation in which abstract principles are sacrificed to doctrines of expediency, — particularly as exemplified in the case of the experiment in the British West Indies; and lastly, to suggest a plan which shall reconcile the claims of each party, in so far as those claims are equitable, and which, avoiding the errors of British legislation, shall be capable of immediate adoption, without involving the anomalous spectacle of a measure righteous in itself leading to calamitous results.

I am, Sir,
Your faithful Servant,
M. B. SAMPSON.

Clapham New Park, Surrey, England,
4th November, 1844.

SECTION I.

OF THE INTERESTS INVOLVED IN THE ABOLITION OF SLAVERY, AND THE EXTENT TO WHICH THEY SHOULD BE REGARDED.

THE interests alleged to be opposed to the abolition of Slavery are,—the Slave-owners individually; the States, whose productive power would be destroyed; and the Slave population itself, which is now controlled and provided for, but which, from a state of freedom, would fast retrograde into barbarism.

1. The claim of the Slave-owner to his right of property is often met by a bold denial. It is alleged that no law can constitute one man the property of another, and in the abstract this is correct. But it is possible for a State to make an unjust law, and having thus tempted individuals into error, it cannot escape, when it sees the wrong which it has committed, from its liability to make amends to those whom it has misled. The Slave-owner, when his legal title is threatened, will plead that, in passing the law which gave it to him, the State did not seek his individual profit, but its own; that no higher exercise of intelligence or morality could have been expected from him than that which has been manifested by the collective wisdom of his countrymen; and that the act to which a legal sanc-

tion had been given, was hardly likely to strike his mind as an improper one; that he does not profess to be wiser or better than others, and that even on points where he has doubts, he might be led to discard them through faith in the better judgment of the majority; that in all his social relations he has only sought to satisfy himself that he was acting in obedience to the laws, and that he never dreamed he could be legally punished for an act which, at the time of its performance, was not recognised as a crime. For the State to take from him a legal title which, for its own purposes, it voluntarily gave, and for which it permitted him to give a consideration, is undeniably a punishment, and one the injustice of which becomes more apparent, when it is recollected that the title was not only given, but promised to be maintained, so that any individual, or body of individuals attempting to deprive him of it should be severely punished.

If we were to arrive at the conclusion that all laws may be abrogated the moment they are discovered to be unjust, without providing compensation to those who, acting under them, have parted with their money, there is very little property in the world that could be regarded as secure. To one diffident in his own judgment, and unable, in all cases, even with an earnest desire, to ascertain the true path, it would be no guide that he is supported by the law. "It sanctions such and such a course to-day," he might reflect, " and if I invest my money I am told that it will be safe, that my title will be good, and that those who deprive me of it will be punished. But I am not able to determine its inherent morality; to-morrow the State may discover that it is wrongly-founded, and I may be a ruined man." It is considered by many that the largest portion of the National Debt of Great Britain was contracted to carry on unjust wars, for which the future energies of the people were recklessly pledged; but even if the impolicy and injustice of these wars were universally admitted, no one would think of visiting upon the individual lender the consequences arising from the errors of the State. The majority of the mind of England gave sanction to them, and the same majority must provide the means of meeting their disagreeable results.

But it may be urged that, admitting the liability of the State, where there are two parties to an unjust transaction, the one should bear the same proportion as the other. That the Slave-owner and the Government should divide the loss. This argument, however, will not hold good. It is the law itself which is unjust; the after acts of individuals are merely its inevitable consequences. The question, therefore, simply is, what share had the Slave-owner in the framing and maintenance of the law which declared negroes to be " property," and what is to be his consequent proportion of the loss to be sustained by its abolition. His share was precisely that of an individual, and nothing further, and all that he can be called upon to bear is his proportion of such tax as may be necessary to defray the compensation to be given. Each member of the aggregate body by whom the investment of capital in Slave-holding was sanctioned, is liable to the same responsibility as the one who acted on that sanction.

The best way in all cases to ascertain the duty of a State, is to see what it would be just for an individual to do under like circumstances. The State is merely the representative of the justice of the many. It says to individuals, "We take power out of your hands, because if you were permitted to use it, you would be swayed by personal feelings, which would cause you to act dishonestly. If you could set those feelings aside, and deal to every man justly and impartially, there would be no occasion for a government: but this is out of the question, and a central power must be established, which, owing to its being (as an aggregate of the many) free from private bias, will be able to do in each case what it would be *right* for the individual to do if it were possible to trust him." Whatever, therefore, it is proper to demand from an individual it is, above all, proper to demand from a government.

Now, if a person delegated to represent the interests of the many, and known to possess the best means of collecting information and forming a judgment, were, in the exercise of his discretion, to tempt another to embark money in a particular direction, by undertaking, on behalf of his constituents, to execute a certain title-deed, and to maintain its legality, (it being generally understood that he was entitled to perform such an act,) what course should we require of him, as an honest man, upon his making the discovery that the title he has professed to execute applies to an object to which no legitimate possession can attach—that he had never, in fact, any right to give it, and that it is expedient, therefore, to cancel the whole transaction? Most assuredly he is bound to say to the party whom he has misled, " You paid so much, as the value of the title which you received from me, and the legality of which, as an inducement for you to carry out my views, I promised to maintain. This promise I now find I cannot in conscience keep. I am aware, that in giving it I did not make any reservation in my own behalf; that in undertaking to protect your title against all other parties, I did not reserve the right of depriving you of it myself; nor did I give you leave to suppose that the undertaking was only for a specific period. It was altogether unlimited, and was put forth for the purpose of inducing you to invest your capital in a mode which I believed to have been for the advantage of those whom I represent. I have, therefore, no alternative, in taking back that which I indiscreetly gave, but to pay its market value,—a value upon which you have doubtless based all your proceedings. If I am unable to do this, if I assume the right to break my pledge, and at the same time refuse you an equivalent, of course, for the future I must be prepared to find that my word will be rejected by all men."

Thus then, although the law which constitutes one man the property of another is inherently unjust, it is binding in the country where it exists between the State and individuals. If the State has erroneously recognized such property, and has contracted in good faith, for its own ends, that the right of possession shall be held sacred, it is especially bound in its own person to recognize the obligation, or to make amends for its non-fulfilment.

On the other hand, the relative position of the Slave and his master admits of no discussion. It is founded and maintained in fraud, and fraud only, and of course cannot be recognized by other powers, or by the Slave himself. The inalienable rights of life, liberty, and the pursuit of happiness, have not been so inefficiently upheld by the wise through all the struggles of advancing civilization, as to admit of their appearing among the unsettled questions of the nineteenth century.

In the case of the African, it is sometimes pleaded that his condition is greatly improved by his captivity amongst white men; but this does not palliate the means by which the improvement has been brought about. The condition of a human being who has passed his days in virtue, is raised beyond all conception by his release from this life; but the murderer who helps him to Heaven must not expect on that account to escape retribution.

We must recognize, therefore, the institution of Slavery as sinful without mitigation, and that it is the perfect right of the Slave to break his bonds whenever practicable. It would be well, however, that the acknowledgment of this right should always be accompanied by explanation. The great doctrines upon which is based the argument for emancipation also proclaim the sin of meeting violence by violence. He, therefore, who would instil into the Slave the propriety of resorting to any means inconsistent with a forgiveness even of the tyrant who has most trespassed against him, counsels him to reject the very creed upon which rests the surest hopes of the freedom of his race. There are, I fear, some who profess themselves friends of the slave who will renounce this application of the doctrine; but to the common heart it will commend itself by its simple truth. All attempts to arouse the fears of the Slave-owner by threats or attempts of violence, have only led to increased severities and a stronger dislike of emancipation; while by stimulating the lower feelings of the negro they must have tended to subdue those qualities of his nature by which alone he can permanently hope to defeat the injustice of his oppressors. If it is possible for the slave to escape without fraud or violence, it is his duty to do so,—otherwise it is his duty to submit to his lot, and to regard it as the will of that Being who will requite in his own time, and who has expressly forbidden a return of treachery for treachery, or blow for blow.

2. Having thus considered the interests of the Slave-owner individually, and the extent to which his position is to be respected, we have now to contemplate the effect which the abolition of Slavery would produce upon the interests of the State.

Of the two great arguments commonly used on this head—the danger of a war of races, and the certain ruin which must result from diminished production—the latter only is worthy of attention. It is against all experience to suppose that those who have shown docility and patience under oppression and ill-treatment, will all at once assume an opposite nature when their grievances are removed. The supposition is also at variance with the oft-repeated assertion made by Southern men in defence of Slavery, that the negroes, in their present state, are contented, happy, and well-cared for, and feel a strong affection for the families of their owners. This state of things could only have grown up under a mild rule, and it is therefore vain to allege in the face of it, that the negroes are only kept from attempting to exterminate the whites by the superior force which the latter, by means of the institution of Slavery, are enabled constantly to exercise. It may be said that the advantage consists in the power to check any combination for violent ends; but it would be unreasonable to assume that a race of " contented and affectionate" people are only waiting for the power to combine in order to become discontented and savage; that it is a peculiarity, in fact, of peaceable natures to become fierce and malignant in the aggregate! If, however, reason were not sufficient to decide this point, the example of the British West Indies would be conclusive. In no State of America does the negro population preponderate more over the white than in South Carolina, where it is 335,314 against 259,084, while in British Guiana, in 1834, it was 71,916 against 3006. If the experiment of complete emancipation has taken place safely in Guiana, it may surely be attempted elsewhere without dread;* and, apart from the evidence of the docility of the negro, it must seem a satire upon the white population of the Southern States, to suppose them doubtful of their skill and courage to counteract any possible " combination" of an equal number of that race, whose intellect and energies they have ever held in scorn.

So abundant are the evidences of the feebleness of the blacks, and their generally inactive and submissive spirit, that the argument of *fear*, when urged by the white man, appears to be degrading to the position which he occupies, and one which the advocates of emancipation should therefore treat with utter disregard. The other argument, however, to which I have alluded, the effects of emancipation in causing diminished production, is one of undeniable weight.

* In the Island of Mauritius the population was 8844 white against 84,464 coloured. Of the slaves, about 40,000 are estimated to have been imported Africans, and consequently far less ripe for freedom than those in the other British possessions, or in the United States. Yet this island formed no exception to the general results.

That sudden freedom of choice on the part of the negro between labour and idleness would always be followed, more or less, by a selection of the latter, was a fact easily to be inferred from his physical constitution: nor was it indeed often denied until the ardour of debate occasionally outran discretion. The result of the experiment in the British possessions has at length effectually closed all discussion on the point, and shown that the anticipations of evil in respect to it have a solid foundation.

I recognize this argument, therefore, as possessing great weight, not in opposition to emancipation, but in opposition to any plan of emancipation in which it shall not have been duly considered. It is a simple task to sweep away evils if we are reckless as to those we substitute in their place; but it is the nature of all truly righteous acts to be free from attendant mischief. Now, to the extent that emancipation causes a diminution of labour, it must not only throw land out of cultivation, and produce individual ruin, but deprive a large portion of the inhabitants of the globe of the necessaries of life. The English peasant must pay more for her cotton gown, and the farmer of New York must diminish his consumption of sugar; and although deprivations of this kind may at first sight appear simple, they are certain to produce many disastrous results both on the moral and physical condition of mankind. It will not do, therefore, to exclaim, " Such things are not to be heeded. Our first great duty is to get rid of the crying sin of

Slavery, at all hazards, and without regard to consequences." The Creator has so ordered the world that even here prosperity is a certain result of virtue; and the power of showing that such is the case forms one of our strongest aids in awakening the sordid-minded to His will. If, therefore, in carrying out any measure of duty we act so as to bring injurious consequences immediately in its train, we destroy our most convincing argument to induce others to do likewise. With regard to emancipation in the British colonies, it has been well observed, " An effort must be made to show those tropical countries which still cling to Slavery, that this moral triumph has entailed no counterbalancing sacrifice; that economically, as well as morally, all parties have gained by the change. If this can be done, the slave-holding countries will follow our example from interested motives; and the abolition of Slavery will create that high and delicate sense of the rights of all human beings, which at present does not exist among them, and to which, therefore, we should appeal in vain. On the other hand, if we do not succeed in making free labour at least as available as slave labour, we shall have given to the Slave-owners an additional motive for adhering to Slavery, and, by affording them an advantage over us in the markets of the world, a stimulus to increase the number of their slaves and the activity of the slave-trade." That these results have actually taken place is now matter of history; and it therefore more especially behoves those who may hereafter legislate for the abolition of Slavery to guard against the evil.

If, indeed, we arrive at the conviction that there is no way of stepping from sin but such as in its first effects shall lead to disaster,—that the immediate consequence of a return to obedience must inevitably be bitter—it will of course be our duty to submit to it; but reason and experience combine to show that sacrifices of this kind are not required, and that they only follow as the penalty of our own imperfect plans. In the case of emancipation being effected without any arrangement to prevent a diminution of produce, the poor sugar consumer of civilized countries is exposed to daily privations destructive of health and comfort, which are comparatively unfelt by his wealthy neighbour; and hence a glaring disparity is evident in the distribution of the suffering consequent on the measure. That such a disparity could not arise under the laws of Providence as the necessary working of an arrangement wholly just, will be admitted by all. It is a contingency which the framers of an Emancipation Act are bound to provide against; and the plea that the great end of their plan is a righteous one, will no more justify neglect on this point than it would if we were to bring a man into the open air after we had wrongfully confined him amidst infection, without taking precautions that the act of justice should not cause injury to others. Of course if no party is able to suggest a less imperfect method of carrying out a paramount duty than one which involves a disregard of minor duties, which should be concurrently performed, it is best to act as far as our light will go, but we must not complain when we experience the natural consequences of our want of clear perceptions, nor regard them as unavoidably flowing from obedience to the Divine laws. At the same time, also, we are bound to look with more leniency on those who, under such circumstances, refuse to follow our example, than if instead of rejecting truth in an imperfect form, they could be charged with spurning her when presented to them in her fair proportions.

3. The remaining argument that the welfare of the negro is involved in the continuance of Slavery, since the restraint to which he is subjected is essential to prevent him from falling into barbarism, is wholly unsupported by experience. Even supposing the effects of emancipation to be such as to drive the white population from the country, owing to their inability to render it productive, there is no reason to believe that the condition of the negro in his uncontrolled state would be lower than it is at present. In Hayti, where the most unfavourable circumstances have been presented, the course of the people is still stated to have been one of progress rather than of retrogression, and " the population has been doubled by a natural increase since the establishment of freedom."

It may be said that it is in opposition to the fact of the negro having been raised in the social scale by transportation from freedom in Africa to Slavery in the West, to suppose that his improvement would not be stopped by permitting him, without restriction, to select his own mode of life. But such is not the case. The negro does not advance in Africa, because a pestilential climate keeps all white men from its shores, save those who, by means of the Slave-trade, brutalize the natives, and divert them from the pursuits of industry; but on the continent of America the negro, even if he dwelt in a community of his own, would be brought constantly under the influence of traders and missionaries, and although his improvement would be slow, it would not be suspended. It would proceed, indeed, at a greater pace than can ever be hoped for under Slavery; more especially such Slavery as that which now exists in the United States, where the predominant effort of the master is avowedly to crush the development of all moral or intellectual power. That any condition of unregulated freedom is superior to Slavery is also supported by the fact that the free coloured population of the Southern States (described by Southern orators as occupying the most unfavourable position in which the African race could by any possibility be placed) show a duration of life far exceeding that of their servile brethren.

But although the argument of the maintenance of Slavery being desirable for the welfare of the negro is wholly untenable, it must be admitted that any plan of emancipation will prove vitally defective which fails to provide the certainty of his steady and rapid advance. The condition of the people of St. Domingo and Liberia, although it may be one of progress, is certainly not such as to present to slave-holding countries any very striking conception of the injury they inflict upon the race by withholding from them their liberty; nor can the act of unriveting their chains, and permitting them to vegetate in freedom, be regarded as a fulfilment of what is due for three centuries of wrong. However gratifying might be the act of Abolition, it would be a bitter disgrace to a civilized people to permit it to be accompanied by the avowal that with all their intelligence they are unable to devise a means to avert the disastrous idleness which threatens to result from it, and which, by preventing any satisfactory advance of the long-injured race, if not by leading to their actual deterioration, would rob the measure of its brightest fruits. For any plan, therefore, to be thoroughly welcome to the friend of the negro, it is essential that it should provide against the danger of his falling into that degree of sloth, the proverbial root of all evil, which would impede his progress in civilization; and although the want of power to suggest such a provision is not to be admitted as an argument against the demand for immediate emancipation any more than the want of power to devise a preventive for the falling off of the productive capabilities of the country, it would, as in that case, show the friends of emancipation to be but indifferently prepared to fulfil one of the chief duties which the act involves, and that a further palliation might therefore be offered for the resistance directed against their efforts.

The conditions which the foregoing considerations present as essential to any successful plan for the Abolition of Slavery, are:—

1st, That it shall provide full compensation from the State to each individual Slave-owner.

2nd, That it shall not compromise the prosperity of the State, by causing a diminution of its productive power.

And lastly, That means shall be taken to prevent the negro from sinking into slothfulness, and to repair the injustice of the past by zealous efforts to develope his energies and raise him in the social scale.

Of these, the provision for compensation to the Slave-owner is to be regarded as absolutely indispensable; the other two are so far essential that the neglect of them would amount to neglect of obvious duties, and would consequently involve severe calamities: but they differ from the first, inasmuch as if we were unable to see our way to enforce them, this inability would not justify a moment's delay in relinquishing the sin of slavery. It would amount to a grievous omission, a want of prudence and foresight, but not to the committal of a direct wrong. But in carrying out emancipation by a direct breach of faith with the planter, we should merely be substituting one wrong for another; and although the new sin may be apparently less than that which it displaces—although we do a small evil that a great good may come—we must remember that in no case is it permitted for us to seek our ends by conduct of this description. So long as we do not see that we can work towards the good we desire by wholly unexceptionable means, we may be sure that we have not yet hit upon the true path, and that it is our duty still to pause—not in apathy, but with an earnest seeking for direction, and the assurance that our efforts will be rewarded. It is therefore better that Slavery should not be abolished, than that it should be abolished by denying compensation, because this would amount to the sin of acknowledging sufficient light to recognize the laws of God, and daring, while in possession of it, to assert that they can be worked out by fraudulent designs.

The eagerness to carry out a favourite point by measures, of the perfect justness of which we entertain a doubt, is a sure way to retard our final aim. That justice cannot be inconsistent with itself, that there must be some way of redressing every evil which shall be free from injury to any human being, should always be borne in mind, and each scheme rejected, until that one is presented which satisfies the conscience as being consistent with integrity to all. If we o'erleap these points, and professing to serve Heaven, offend, for the sake of "expediency," in the slightest degree against our sense of duty, we destroy that coherency which can alone give strength and beauty to our plan, and introduce at once the elements of its ruin.

SECTION II.

OF THE MEASURES HITHERTO TAKEN FOR THE ABOLITION OF SLAVERY.

HAVING considered the points to be provided for in any measure which may be proposed for the Abolition of Slavery, it is proper to review the means which have already been taken or suggested by the United States or other nations for their accomplishment. If we can find in any quarter that the difficulties connected with them have been fairly met and overcome, the trouble of further inquiry will be spared, and America can have no pretext for a single moment to delay emancipation. If, however, only a portion of them have been got over, the task still devolves upon us of providing for the remainder; while, if none can be shown to have been successfully grappled with, we shall have to discard all consideration of what has already been proposed or adopted—useful only as a warning—and to suggest an independent plan.

The British Emancipation Act, of 1833, stands forth as the measure upon the success of which the progress of emancipation in other slave-holding countries was considered greatly to depend. Depraved as mankind may be, no doubt can exist that the majority, if unperverted by false fears of damage to themselves, would prefer to show kindness instead of cruelty to their fellow-men; and it was therefore reasonable to entertain a certain trust, that if the measure adopted by Great Britain should be found to produce or threaten no injurious consequences, it would, after a fair trial, be speedily imitated by other nations. Such imitation has, however, in no single instance taken place. Eleven years have passed, and although the friends of emancipation in the United States and elsewhere, have used their constant efforts to hold up the example of Great Britain, and to pourtray in the brightest terms the results of her experiment, the feeling on the question, so far from having advanced, has undergone a most unfavourable change, and the prospects of the coloured race are less hopeful now than at any former period. The inquiry suggests itself, Can this effect have arisen from the working of a judicious measure, or is it the natural consequence of attempting to achieve a good end by unjust and imperfect means? and an examination as to how far the British Act was framed in accordance with the conditions which, in the preceding section, have been shown to be essential to success, will lead us to an answer.

These conditions required that provision should be made for compensation to the planter, for the maintenance of the productive power of the country, and for the certain advancement of the coloured population.

There appear to me to be few instances of more fatal delusion than that which is nursed by the people of England regarding the compensation voted by Parliament to the parties interested in this question. From the commencement of the debates by which that vote was preceded, down to the present time, a constant outpouring of self-gratulation has always attended any reference to the matter. It was originally announced as " a costly sacrifice," widely spoken of in the House of Commons as a " lavish sum," a " munificent gift," " an instance of magnanimity such as never occurred before," &c., and universally admitted out of doors, and even by foreign nations, as a " noble vindication of the right of property." Subsequently it has been described not only by ardent abolitionists, but by political economists as " a measure reflecting quite as much credit on the wisdom and honesty as on the generosity of the British Nation;" and these ideas (too agreeable to the national vanity to stimulate any very close questioning from less informed persons) meeting with universal reception, have led to a belief not only that our past sins in connexion with Slavery have been effectually wiped out, but that England is entitled to boast of her singular virtue, and to cast stones at those countries which refuse to imitate her example.

A little consideration would dissipate this error. It must readily be perceived that the Act of Emancipation was nothing more than an act to provide for the abandonment of a heinous sin, in which the State of Great Britain had through a long period indulged; and that even if its provisions had been framed in perfect wisdom and justice, the spirit in which it should have been adopted was that of deep humiliation for the past, together with a sense that in merely abstaining from a continuance in wickedness, we could certainly acquire no right to boast of having done anything to claim the especial praises of our fellow-men. Under the most favourable circumstances, therefore, the subdued tone of sincere repentance would have been alone appropriate, coupled with that patient interpretation of the sins of others which a newly awakened consciousness of our own enormities is calculated to beget. But the mode in which the claim for compensation was dealt with, was not such as to entitle us even to the amount of gratification which might thus have been enjoyed, since it was characterized by features of injustice, showing too plainly that we were not prepared to effect our withdrawal from the sin of Slavery without committing a new infringement of the moral law.

In bringing forward his plan, Lord Stanley (then Mr. Secretary Stanley,) having distinctly recognized the claim of the planters to full compensation for the withdrawal of their legal title to property in the coloured race, took as his estimate of the value of that property the sum of thirty millions sterling, being 800,000 slaves at 37*l*. 10*s*. each; and the way in which he proposed to meet this amount was by a direct payment of twenty millions, and by continuing to the holders a right of property in the labour of the negroes for periods (according to their class as predial or non-predial) of twelve and seven years, the value of such labour being considered as equivalent to the balance. It will be seen from this that the Government, after admitting the utter sinfulness of Slavery, refused to abolish it at once, and entered into a sort of composition; they were willing to incur a certain expense, but could not summon resolution to meet the full amount. Thirty millions being required, they could make up their minds to go as far as twenty; and to raise the remaining ten, they resolved to rob the negro of his labour for a further period of twelve years. It is. true, a pretext was urged for this course, that " immediate emancipation would be no less ruinous to the slave than to the master;" and that the period for the prolongation of Slavery "under the specious title of apprenticeships, where nothing was to be learned, and no wages were to be paid," was alleged to be necessary as a probation. But, even if we admit the necessity of enforcing the labour of the negro for a certain term preparatory to complete emancipation, it is difficult to see how it justifies the appropriation of the value of that labour. The work might have been enforced so as to keep up the industry and discipline of the negroes, while the ten millions, at which it was estimated, might have been paid over to them; or if it had been deemed dangerous to place them suddenly in possession of money, it might have been reserved for their benefit at some future period. Apart from this, however, the plea for the necessity of the apprenticeship, as far as regarded a large class of the negroes (if not the whole of them), was shown at the time to be completely untenable, for no one attempted to assert that the class of artificers and mechanics were not fit for instant liberty. Although, therefore, it may be admitted that as respects two-thirds of the required payment, the British Government were disposed to act honestly, it is obvious that the "noble example of the maintenance of the right of property," as far as it was involved in the remaining third, was to be upheld only at the expense of the coloured race.

Still, under this arrangement—supposing the estimate of the value of the Slaves at thirty millions to have been fairly made — the compensation to the planters would have been complete, however questionable the means of raising it. If it had been carried out, no question, as far as the strict maintenance of the right of property amongst ourselves was concerned, it could have been raised; and although reproach would still have attached to the Government, it would have arisen simply from the fact that after having sinned for upwards of two centuries, upon awakening at last to a sense of their guilt, they had thought it better to continue sinning for twelve years longer than to increase their payment of twenty millions to thirty. The doctrine promulgated by this line of conduct being, that it is inexpedient to pursue virtue at all costs, and that there is a point at which a continuance in wickedness may be permitted by Providence to prove more profitable than a departure from it.

But the *full* compensation declared by the Minister to be due, was not destined to be paid even in this or any other form. During the progress of the debate, the advocates of the negro succeeded in showing that there was no just ground, even as a matter of safety, for prolonging the state of Slavery, under the title of apprenticeship, for the periods proposed; and Lord Stanley, finding that he could not carry the measure if he persisted in that prolongation, reduced the periods from twelve and seven years to seven years and five. The question naturally arises, In what way was this reduction made up to the Slave-owner? The Minister had stated that " he had considered the period of apprenticeship to be part of the compensation paid to the proprietor," and it is evident that upon a reduction of this part, it became necessary that an increase should be made in some other way. To the consequent interrogatory " Whether, as he had reduced the period of apprenticeship, he intended to increase the compensation?" a simple reply in the negative was given, Government having previously admitted the breach of faith, by announcing that " They had strenuously endeavoured to perform their portion of the engagement; but from the claims made upon them it became impossible, notwithstanding their utmost exertions, to carry it into effect." Having no choice but to break their pledge, or to resign, they determined on the former course; and of just so much compensation as was represented by the term of apprenticeship taken off, the proprietors were consequently defrauded.

Thus then upon the confession of the Minister this very measure of compensation, so universally quoted as a noble instance of national integrity, was marked by a breach of faith which has few parallels in modern legislation. The proceeding, indeed, was so flagrant, that no excuses were attempted; and it was evidently the nearly unanimous feeling of Parliament that it had better be suffered to pass unnoticed. It was seen that a call for the sum necessary to make up the thirty millions would meet with universal opposition, and no one was prepared with a plan by which justice might have been satisfied without so fearful a drain upon the resources of the country; a drain which, owing to the system of taxation, must have fallen chiefly on the industrious classes. Although, therefore, every member must have felt that the sum awarded was an unjust sum—that the proprietors were entitled to nothing or to more, the injustice, in the eagerness to gain a certain end, was wilfully overlooked, and evil was deliberately sanctioned that good might come.

It will, perhaps, be alleged that the fact of the planters having consented to receive the compensation awarded, shows that no breach of faith can be considered to have taken place, the two parties being entitled to make what bargain they pleased. But this plea is denied, because the planters were not left to their own free action, but driven by intimidation to accept the terms proposed. The Government were aware that by the discussion of emancipation the expectations of the coloured population had become excited to a pitch at which disappointment would have proved dangerous, that the unreflecting masses in England were determined also to have the measure passed without inquiring very rigidly into the means, and that consequently if the planters refused what was offered, they would, as the excitement increased, have to be content with less. The intimidation thus created proved sufficient to induce the consent of the West India interest, and also perhaps to impress them with gratification at having got off so well: but there is evidence that this gratification was only such as is felt by men who, having fallen into powerful and unscrupulous hands, find that by giving up a portion of their property they will be permitted to escape with the remainder.

So notorious was the existence of this intimidation, that unreproved references to the advantages to be derived from it were of constant occurrence during the debates. " Wait for a little period," urged some members, " and a fourth of the money will be quite sufficient;" and one member more ardent than the rest, after connecting the " growing intelligence " of the people with a probability of their " sponging off the national debt," animated by the advantage which the Government had already taken of the fears of those with whom they had to deal, urged it very naturally as a plea for further spoliation. "We had a contest with Ministers the other day, and what has been the result? They yielded. Was ever such conduct witnessed on the part of any Ministry before? Did not Ministers pledge themselves to the West India body to give them twenty millions and twelve years' apprenticeship? and yet after that contest, they the next day, without notice, came to a decision to take off six years of that term; and the West India interest gave in, for they were afraid. But if you on this side of the House will be but united as you ought to be—if one hundred and fifty of you will but stand by one another, I will be bound that the Ministers will give up everything."

In condemning the breach of faith which was thus practised on the Slave-owner, it is not necessary to overlook the misconduct of his class. In no case can the character of the party with whom we have to deal bear in the slightest degree upon a question of right, save that it is necessary for us to act with more scrupulous fairness in our dealings with the corrupt than with the virtuous, inasmuch as any deviation into which we might fall would be attributed by the upright to unintentional error, while by the unprincipled it would be perpetuated as an example. It was urged amidst the many unweighed suggestions which abounded on all sides, that the planters should be deprived of compensation on account of their having broken their engagement to assist in promoting the Ministerial scheme. This scheme was agreed to be carried out by the Government on the understanding that the planters should co-operate; and if the planters failed to perform this part of their engagement, the Ministers were obviously at liberty to cancel the entire bargain. But the cancelment of a bargain to work out emancipation by a particular method, could give them no right to do more than change it for some other method, consistent with honesty (which of course might be adopted independently of the consent of the planters), or else to leave the question undisturbed. In the House of Commons, however, an opinion seemed prevalent that because the planters had agreed upon a certain mode of giving up a legal right, and had afterwards failed to fulfil their part of the agreement, it became just for the Government to take that right from them by force, although in the contract there was no stipulation for such a penalty.

Having shown that the course pursued by Great Britain regarding compensation cannot be taken as an example by other nations, the Government, notwithstanding their immense resources, having been either incapable or unwilling to grant its full amount; the next step will be to examine if her plan of emancipation included that which is to be regarded as the second element of success;—viz: a due provision for the maintenance of the productive power of the country.

That a reduction in the work performed by the negroes would be the result of emancipation, unless some measures could be designed to avert it, was foreseen by the British Government: and the plan adopted to meet the evil was, as we have seen, the establishment of a period of apprenticeship or modified Slavery preparatory to complete abolition. Into the provisions of this plan it is unnecessary to enter, its failure having been so complete as to lead to its discontinuance in the various colonies on the 1st of August, 1838. At that period, therefore, the negro was suffered to come into possession of unrestricted freedom, without any further method having been devised by the Government for guarding against his withdrawal from steady labour. The consequences of this neglect in diminishing the productive power of the West India colonies were such, to use the words of a Report of a Committee of the House of Commons on West Africa, as to give "an extraordinary stimulus to the Slave-trade for the supply of Cuba and Brazil," and the extent to which the diminution of produce took place will be shown by the following tables:—

QUANTITIES OF PRODUCE IMPORTED INTO GREAT BRITAIN FROM THE YEAR 1831 TO 1843, BOTH INCLUSIVE.

Years.	Population.	Sugar.	Molasses.	Rum.	Coffee.	Cocoa.
		cwt.	cwt.	galls.	lbs.	lbs.
1831	Slaves. 800,000	4,103,800	323,306	7,844,157	20,030,802	1,491,947
1832	,,	3,773,456	553,663	4,713,809	24,673,920	618,215
1833	,,	3,646,205	686,794	5,109,975	19,008,375	2,125,656
1834	Apprentices. 769,000	3,843,976	650,366	5,112,400	22,081,490	1,360,355
1835	,,	3,524,209	507,495	5,453,317	14,852,470	439,447
1836	,,	3,601,791	526,535	4,868,168	18,903,426	1,612,304
1837	,,	3,306,775	575,657	4,418,349	15,577,888	1,847,145
1838	Freemen. 750,000	3,520,676	638,007	4,641,210	17,588,655	2,149,637
1839	,,	2,824,372	474,307	4,021,820	11,485,675	959,641
1840	,,	2,214,764	424,141	3,780,979	12,797,739	2,374,301
1841	,,	2,151,217	430,221	2,770,161	9,927,689	2,920,298
1842	,,	2,508,552	471,737	3,823,128	9,186,555	2,490,597
1843	,,	2,502,591	605,611	2,802,138	8,251,892	1,496,554

On this head it has been remarked:* " The extent to which the quantity of produce annually raised in the British sugar colonies was reduced, and the cost of production enhanced by emancipation, is startling to contemplate. The decrease in production was not confined to sugar; it extended to all the staple products of these colonies; and it can be shown that it was occasioned by the consequences of emancipation alone.

" It has been proved by the evidence given to the West-India Committee of the House of Commons, that from 1837 to 1840, in British Guiana much less work was done in every stage of cultivation; that production had fallen off, and some estates had been put out of cultivation. In Trinidad the difficulty of procuring continuous labour was such, that Mr. Burnley assured the committee, were he proprietor of every estate in the island he would throw the half out of cultivation, convinced that he could produce more by concentrating the work of the available labourers on the rest. In Jamaica the produce of the large estates was reduced one half, and the estates of the poorer proprietors were entirely deserted by the labourers. In Grenada no estates had been actually thrown out of cultivation, but the crops had been so diminished that the result was much the same."

It will thus be seen that, as far as regards the second point to be provided for, the British measure of

* Spectator, 15 April, 1843.

emancipation affords no safe example; and it now only remains for us to inquire if it gives any guiding light upon the third point, viz.; the duty of providing for the certain advancement of the coloured population.

That a great advance has taken place in the intellectual and moral condition of the negroes in some of the West India Islands, from the date of the Emancipation Act, must be admitted by all who will consult the various statements put forth since that time. In Jamaica, the calm and cheerful anticipations which grew out of the reports of their admirable conduct on the 1st of August, 1838—the opening day of freedom—have been more than fulfilled; and there is ground to believe that under a continuance of favourable circumstances a degree of civilization would be reached, in which they would not suffer by comparison with the labouring classes of other countries.

The progress which has thus taken place may be attributed to the faithful efforts of their religious teachers, and to the vigilance of the Home Government in enforcing the fair working of the new system. The Emancipation Act itself made no actual provision for the advancement of the negro, but merely set him free to work out his own progress, and to conquer the effects of past ill-usage. The results, therefore, as far as they have gone, will probably be quoted to show that nothing more was necessary; but a little reflection will satisfy us that such an argument would not hold good, and that the course of Great Britain has been as short-sighted upon this point as upon those we have already considered.

If the negro has already advanced morally and intellectually, so as to fulfil all ordinary anticipations, what more, it will be asked, can be required? It is plain that this state of things would be perfectly satisfactory, with one proviso, viz.; the certainty that it is not a merely temporary progress, but such as will be steadily maintained.

This certainty is wholly wanting, and there is evidence that the prospect is of the most precarious kind. No effective mode having been devised by the Government to ensure the constant industry of the negroes, their labour since 1838 has only been attained at an enormous cost, and in an uncertain manner. It is true that the acquisitive propensity strongly marks their character; but the activity of this one impulse has not proved sufficient to overcome, even partially, their constitutional indolence, except when stimulated to a great degree. The consequence is, that the rate of wages, even for such labour as can be obtained, is so high as to render it impossible for the West India planter to compete either with the slave or free produce of other countries; and although, even under the recent alteration of the sugar duties, an amount of about a million and a quarter sterling will annually be paid as protection on that article alone, we are told that, without larger sacrifices on the part of the mother country, it will be impossible for the proprietors to continue cultivation. At a public meeting at Anatto Bay, on the 19th of June last, resolutions were passed affirming that, under existing circumstances, "the colonies are doomed to ultimate ruin," and that the inhabitants (both white and coloured) " scarcely know whether to surrender themselves to despair, or to attempt to remonstrate with the Government." It is added also, that the approaching necessity for the abandonment of estates " will cut off all prospect of civilization for the children of Africa, and thus entail a curse more grievous and deplorable, if possible, than the curse of slavery—the curse of savage existence and enduring barbarism." Again : " A proprietor," under date the 8th of July, alluding to the recent measures, writes from Grenada, " As things *were*, men fancied they might struggle on, in the hope that better times might come round; but now *all* hope is destroyed:" while from other quarters anticipations of the same gloomy nature have been forcibly proclaimed. It must be admitted as probable, that these statements, although they coincide with the representations of the West India body in the House of Commons, greatly exaggerate the evils to be apprehended, and that the present amount of protection will prove sufficient to prevent an abandonment of cultivation; but they serve to confirm a very general impression, that no great reduction could take place without endangering this end, and that upon the continuance therefore of an enormous annual sacrifice the welfare of the negro depends.

" If, under the difficulties of the present crisis," says Mr. Gurney in his " Winter in the West Indies," " the prohibitory duties on slave-grown coffee and sugar should be relaxed or extinguished, a market of immense magnitude would immediately be opened for the produce of the slave labour of the Brazils, Cuba, and Porto Rico. The consequence would be, that ruin would soon overtake the planters of our West Indian colonies, and our free negroes would be deprived of their principal means of obtaining an honourable and comfortable livelihood."

Now when we consider that the cost of this protection presses chiefly upon the poorer classes of England, it is impossible to avoid the apprehension that it may not always be patiently submitted to. At all events, little can be said for the wisdom or justice of a Government which has left the civilization of the coloured race to be dependent on the maintenance of an artificial price for one of the chief necessaries of life—an article equally in demand by the rich and the poor, and of which the free use is absolutely essential as a preventive of serious diseases.

Symptoms of impatience have already been widely manifested. " The high price of colonial produce," writes Mr. Oldfield, "for the last few years, has created throughout the country a very general feeling against the prohibitory duties upon the sugar and coffee of Brazils and Cuba;" and in one of the London journals the case has been strongly put. In allusion to the rate of wages demanded in the West Indies, and to Mr. Gurney's description of the condition of the labourers, it is remarked—" The truth is, the negroes are in the flourishing condition described by Mr. Gurney, because almost the whole of the price paid for sugar goes into their pockets. The people of England will not long endure this. When they hear of the luxurious negroes, they will say, 'We paid twenty millions to make them free; but we will not always submit to pay for the sugar they make, by working thirty hours a week, a price which enables them to enjoy the luxuries of the middle class at home, while our English labourers, by a week's work of more than twice as many hours, can barely earn a subsistence.' "

That the moral and religious advancement of the negroes should comprise, in order to insure its permanence, strict habits of frugality and industry, will scarcely be denied. It is impossible, however, to read of labour for thirty hours per week being "sufficient to provide comforts and luxuries to an extent not known by any peasantry in the world," without seeing that a state of things exists to beget rather than to overcome a dislike to continued toil. When we meet, therefore, with descriptions of their handsome wedding-dresses, the eggs consumed for their wedding cakes, the wine in their cottages, the mules and horses on which they come riding to their chapels, their champagne, and their pic-nic dinners, so far from being struck with gratifying evidence of a growing civilization, we become impressed with the idea of a class of persons cruelly placed by defective legislation in a false position. It is no reproach to the negro that he does not work more continuously. In a country where twenty-six days' work during the year is sufficient to supply food for the labourer and his family, it would be difficult, even if he possessed the energy of a European, to prevent him from falling into idleness, unless some motive could be awakened in addition to those which ordinarily operate. He has been placed in a position which even the British or Anglo-American labourer would be unable to resist, and which must inevitably unfit him to submit cheerfully to the low rate of remuneration which, under natural circumstances, is paid for unskilled labour in every other part of the world; a rate to which he must nevertheless approach, or be abandoned to self-government, whenever his present artificial condition shall be disturbed.

Although in the foregoing considerations we have looked only to the effects of emancipation on the moral condition of Jamaica, and some other islands where they present the most favourable aspect, we find them fraught with alarming probabilities. The worst anticipations may therefore be entertained for the fate of those communities where, owing to a higher rate of wages, the necessity for prolonged industry is less. From evidence collected by the Agricultural and Immigration Society of Trinidad three years after full emancipation, it appeared that in that island an active labourer " could easily save six or seven dollars per week;" but that, although it was possible even for women to perform three "tasks" a day with ease, " very few of the labourers performed two tasks, many only three or four in the week, and some not more than one;" that plunder of canes was carried on to a great extent, and could not be checked, because the planters were afraid the labourers in such case would leave their work and go elsewhere; that the greater number squandered their earnings in " drinking, gambling, and dissipation;" that so far from employing their spare time in raising provisions and small stock, " produce of that kind had fallen off," owing to the carelessness caused by high wages; and, finally, that the labour actually performed was " dirty and slovenly, and infinitely worse than it was in the time of slavery." It may be urged that some of this evidence came from questionable, because interested, sources; but it found confirmation from other quarters: and even if only partially correct, it must lead to conclusions of a very unfavourable kind. It was shown on the most reliable testimony that " drinking was becoming more prevalent even amongst the women," and that the habit threatened " in two or three years to demoralize the whole labouring population;" that the vice of gambling was increasing also every day; that " instead of improvement in agriculture, everything had retrograded;" and that although no peasantry in the world were so well able to pay for the education of their children, they showed " the greatest reluctance to incur the expense."

In the third case, then, as in the others, no due precautions were either adopted or suggested; and it will therefore appear, that in all the points essential to the success of emancipation, the British measure was deficient, and that it must consequently be discarded from the consideration of those who desire to promote in other countries the freedom of the coloured race. It is not unsatisfactory to arrive at this conclusion, because, if the measure could be shown to have been sound, the fact of its not having been imitated by other nations would present a sadder augury than need now be entertained.

Nor can those who refer to the opinions and motives avowed on this question in the British Parliament feel surprise at the failure of their counsels. At an early stage of the discussion, Lord Stanley took occasion explicitly to deprecate a consistent adherence to principle. Recognizing the experiment as one " more mighty, as well as more important and more interesting in its results, than any experiment ever attempted to be carried into effect by any nation in any period of the history of the world," his lordship deemed it impossible to be carried through without sacrificing " some of those abstract principles — those wild, though benevolent theories," which are founded on the great rule of conscience, that you have no right to keep any man subject to any conditions except such as are imposed upon him by the laws of nature.

It was particularly sought to impress upon Parliament at the outset that they were " dealing with realities, and not with abstract principles," although it was omitted to be shown what light other than that derived from abstract principles should guide them in dealing with anything. It was as if the Minister had said, " We are about to deliberate with a view to avert evils which we have drawn upon our heads by disobedience of primary laws;—we seek to proclaim to other nations that we now recognize those laws; and this attempt, more important and interesting in its results than any other in the history of the world, requires for its practical and safe operation that on minor points those laws should be disobeyed. It is vain to allege that while the very foundation of our measure consists in the assertion of an abstract principle, it is inconsistent to urge a departure from abstract principles in carrying it out. Arguments of this nature are wild, inexpedient, and unstatesmanlike. The government of the world is so ordered, that while a departure from abstract principles, on a great scale, inevitably brings the severest penalties, an infringement on minor points is often attended with the best results." The views on this head expressed by the proposer of the measure met with ready sympathy from those whom it was his business to conciliate; the only difficulty being such as must inevitably arise in all similar cases,—namely, that although the various speakers uniformly recognized the propriety of an occasional departure from principle, each of them seemed to differ as to the direction in which that departure should be permitted.

It is not, indeed, clear that the Government acted distinctly, even at starting, upon any principle whatever; for while, on the one hand, the Minister referred to the measure as an act of "justice and humanity," which was imperatively called for, even though it would be attended with economical disasters, thereby recognizing those principles as his sole motive, he afterwards constantly alluded to it as a "great boon," and even boasted that "the Government had not called upon the negro to pay any part of the debt *which he owed to the State for his freedom.*" From this it is evident that while the Government at times recognized the inherent claim of the negro, it was at other times felt that no such claim existed, and that emancipation therefore was a piece of liberality by no means absolutely called for. On the opposition side it was also evident that little advance had been made towards a comprehension of the moral argument on which the claim for freedom solely rests. Sir Robert Peel could not recognize it, but thought that liberty should be sold to the negroes, and wished Great Britain to take a lesson from Spain. "He did think it possible that by adopting, on a large scale, the principle of the Spanish law—by holding out to the slave, as a stimulus to labour, the prospect of emancipating himself gradually by the produce of it, by aiding that produce, when it reached a certain amount, by a grant out of the public treasury, we should be promoting the most advantageous measure. If we had lain down the principle of aiding the slaves, by a grant a long way short of twenty millions, to purchase their freedom by their own labour, it would have been more for the interest of the slave than the course we were then pursuing."

On the other hand, those who distinctly recognized the claim of the negro, and were, in this respect, able to comprehend and distinctly act upon a principle, showed that on other points they were not equally inflexible, and that while they clamoured for a strict adherence to the moral law in one direction, they were willing to sacrifice it in another. Thus, while the Government admitting the claim of the planter to full compensation, permitted themselves to depart from principle by granting a lower amount than they had acknowledged to be due, the friends of the negro, contended that the planters were not entitled to any compensation, and that the payment of it was a fraud upon the people of England, voting for it at the same time in all its alleged injustice for the sake of getting freedom for the slave. On all sides the readiness to concede principle—to arrive, in fact, at a desired end by improper means—was unequivocally manifested.

That a measure entered into with such feelings should bring disappointment to its promoters, is consolatory to the friends of truth; for, if it had yielded any other result, it would have swept away the only doctrine by which they are sustained. So long as we can rely that the world is governed by consistent laws, and take our stand on the great principle, that no departure from them—however expedient to a narrow vision it may appear—can bring in the end anything but disaster, we have a rule by which to regulate our course amidst every wavering influence around us; but, if in any case we admit that an abandonment of this principle is advisable, that truth is not coherent, and that a great good may sometimes be helped by a little wrong, we at once plunge into confusion; recognizing the future as depending upon our own dexterity, instead of upon immutable laws, operating solely according to our present obedience. If this were to be admitted, if the statesman's plea of the necessity of unjust expedients—urged to cover his own personal incapacity to act without them—could be shown, even in one instance, to have been warranted by the result, the hopes of advancement, founded on the belief that mankind will at last learn the *invariable* connexion of disaster with injustice, would instantly be extinguished. The whole history of the world has hitherto tended to confirm these hopes; and it is because they would have been destroyed by a different result, that the failure of the British plan of emancipation may be regarded with satisfaction.

It will, perhaps, be alleged, that in the foregoing considerations too much importance has been attached to existing and coming evils, since, although they are of undoubted magnitude, they admit of an easy remedy; that this remedy has already been recognized, and put in train for adoption; and that if it had been made part of the original plan, no difficulties would have arisen.

Now, we are entitled to believe that there are few errors which, even in the darkest hour, may not be retrieved by those who sincerely set about the task; and I am therefore far from denying, in the present instance, that a remedy is to be found. But, inasmuch as the leading members of the British Senate, by whom the original measure was sanctioned, have not yet manifested a sense that its failure arose out of their departure from the straight path, it is to be feared that any remedy that may at present find favour in their eyes will hardly be such as to enable them to regain it. On the surface, therefore, there is nothing to inspire confidence; but it is, nevertheless, proper that we should pause, to enter into a short examination of the schemes proposed.

The most unpromising feature of these schemes consists in their showing a total misconception of the cause of the evil which they are intended to cure. This evil, whatever it may be, cannot originate in the smallness of the population in the West Indies, because the distress now complained of has arisen solely from emancipation; and emancipation, while it has not reduced the number of coloured inhabitants, has actually doubled their working capacity, owing to the fact — that the labour of a free man, when it is fairly brought out, is twice as productive as that of the slave. It is evident, therefore, that the evil has nothing to do with a scarcity of hands, but that it must be looked for in the defective legislation, which permits existing energies to lie dormant.

" The result of our own enquiries," writes Mr. Gurney, in 1840, " is a conviction that the present population of Jamaica, if its force be but fairly applied under a just and wise management, will be found more than adequate to its present extent of cultivation." The schemes, however, to which the British Government have directed their attention, seem based on the idea that the existing distress arises from the want of a sufficient number of labourers, instead of from the absence of a salutary arrangement by which those already in the colonies might be rendered effective; that the problem, in fact, of the superiority of free over slave labour is to be solved by employing an extra number of hands to do the old amount of work, and it is consequently their policy to encourage immigration, even at an enormous outlay. Whatever doubts may attach to this course, as to its effecting the desired end, there might be no objection to the attempt, provided it could be conducted on principles of justice: a short examination, however, will show that there is little prospect of immediate success; and that even if success is temporarily achieved, it will be by measures so completely objectionable as to lead inevitably to ultimate disaster.

The sources whence immigration is looked for are Western Africa and the East Indies. Regarding the first, it has been made evident that if effected to any extent it must be by means little different from those of the slave-trade. Materials for voluntary immigration scarcely exist. The most eligible would be found amongst the Kroomen; and of the chances of success in this quarter, by any honest means, an idea may be gathered from the Report on West Africa, by a Committee of the House of Commons in 1842. " As we proceed up the coast, we fall in, between Cape Palmas and Cape Mount, with a very singular race of men consisting of many small tribes, known commonly by the collective name of Kroomen, scattered along a considerable range of shore; much given, though not exclusively, to maritime pursuits; forming part of the crew of every English man-of-war and merchantman on the coast; known by a distinctive external mark, and neither taken as slaves themselves nor making slaves of others. Their numbers are uncertain, but are undoubtedly considerable, and seem to be increasing; and their confidence in the English character is ascertained. But it seems doubtful whether permission for large numbers to leave their shores could be obtained *without some present to their chiefs;* and their *attachment to their own* *country*, and their present habits of migrating, only for a period and without their families, make it also doubtful whether they would ever become permanent settlers elsewhere, or indeed remain away from home for a longer period than two or three years." The total immigration from Sierra Leone is stated to amount, up to the latest returns, to about 3,297. " To convey these in small detachments, scattered over a space of three years, three first-rate ships have been employed, each having on board a navy lieutenant and surgeon with large salaries." * It must be admitted as probable that private vessels would be more successful than government ships have been; but this would arise from the circumstance that private and interested agents would be infinitely less scrupulous as to the means by which immigrants might be obtained.

So well is it understood that voluntary immigration is not to be managed to any considerable extent that, in 1842, the Agricultural and Immigration Society of Trinidad boldly recommended that the British Government should enter into competition with the slave-buyers on the coast of Africa, and purchase the captive negroes upon condition of their becoming immigrants. " The Committee, therefore," these are their words, " after seriously considering the whole subject, both in its causes and consequences, presume to advise, that if a sufficient number of free labourers are not be found on the coast of Africa

* *Spectator*, 15 June, 1844.

disposed to emigrate to our colonies, some of the unhappy persons who are held there in bondage should be purchased and manumitted for that purpose."

The great plea for resorting to strong measures to induce immigration consists in the advantages that would accrue to the African on being transported to the British colonies—a fact which is dwelt upon by the Committee of the House of Commons with great earnestness. The same plea, however, to a less extent, might have been urged to justify slavery. The question for our consideration is not if the African can be benefited by immigration; but whether, supposing such to be the case, the benefit can be conferred upon him by honest means. The attachment of the negro to his country is well known to be amongst the strongest feelings of his sluggish nature; and it is no more possible to tempt him to leave it by holding out those advantages of civilization which white men consider inducements, than it would have been possible to tempt a Sioux or a Fox to abandon his hunting grounds to partake of the refinements of New York. No doubt we might purchase immigrants upon the plan proposed by the Trinidad Society, to the ultimate advantage of the parties thus acquired; and supposing it to be impossible to set them free in their own land, and at the same time not culpable to become a party—even from good motives—to a trade in human flesh, and also that it was quite certain that for every " unhappy person" so removed some new victim would not be required to fill the gap, the scheme of the Society might perhaps be listened to.

Regarding the second quarter whence immigration is looked for, some striking facts are already before the world. From 1834 to 1838 no fewer than 20,000 Hill Coolies were exported from British India to the Island of Mauritius, with such success, as far as the interests of the planters were concerned in increasing cultivation, as to awaken a strong desire in the West India colonies for a similar advantage; and in July, 1837, an Order in Council was issued by the Government, allowing the importation of Hill Coolies into British Guiana under contracts for a period of five years. Four hundred were accordingly introduced, and a much larger number would have followed, but for a timely exposure of the practices by which these immigrations had been promoted, which caused the authorities to issue a prohibition. From what is understood, however, of the views of the British Government at the present time, it is believed that under certain restrictions the traffic will be largely renewed.*

* The *Times* of the 21st of August last gave insertion to the following :—" HILL COOLIES.—A correspondent informs us that the 10,000 Coolies which Government has allowed to be transported from Calcutta and Madras, are to be sent one half to Demerara, and the remaining 5,000 in equal proportions to Jamaica and Trinidad; these three colonies having given the requisite securities in regard to them. They are to leave the East Indies some time between the months of October and March. Each ship in which they are conveyed must carry a surgeon, and the number of Coolies

The first immigrations to Mauritius were characterized by singular atrocities. In a Despatch to Lord Glenelg, dated the 21st of May, 1839, Sir W. Nicolay says, " That very nefarious practices have been resorted to in many instances in order to procure labourers for embarkation, is beyond all doubt;" and Mr. Anderson, a member of the Committee of Inquiry on Indian Labourers, alleges, that " many of them have been actually kidnapped from their own country, which they have *all* been induced to leave under circumstances of gross fraud."

It is stated, that out of 19,050 Coolies introduced, only 205 were women. Despite the most vigilant watch on board the ships in which they were transported, many suicides were committed. On board one ship, the " Lancier," there appears to have been five, and in another, the " Indian Oak," twelve attempts took place, of which three were successful. The general mortality appears to have been excessive both during the voyage and after their arrival. In British Guiana, also, a dreadful loss of life is stated to have occurred.

in each is to be regulated in terms of the Passengers' Act. It is expected that the cost of transporting them to the West Indies will be about 12*l.* per head. The transport of these, it is thought, will require from 50 to 60 vessels of 400 tons each. It is understood that Government mean to apply to Parliament early next session for an act to permit the introduction of any number of Coolies to the West Indies."—*Greenock Advertiser*.

The last papers received from the West Indies announce that the Demerara legislature have voted, in accordance with the terms of a Despatch from Lord Stanley, 75,000*l.* for the encouragement of Hill Coolie emigration.

The treatment of the labourers by their new masters seems to have been characterized in many instances by the grossest personal violence and injustice; a fact which can hardly cause surprise, when the treatment previously endured by the negroes from the same hands is called to mind, together with the circumstance that after the slave-trade was abolished, the Act of Parliament regarding it was admitted by a Secretary of State to have been violated to no less an extent than 25,000 times by the people of Mauritius.* The fate of an ignorant

* It is difficult to obtain information on which reliance can be placed regarding transactions in Mauritius; but the following paragraph in the *Times* of the 15th of July last tends to confirm existing suspicions, and to show that, after all that has passed, little sense of the duties of humanity has been awakened in that island :—

" The Indian papers brought by the last overland mail record a shocking instance of mortality in a ' Coolie ship,' employed to bring back from Mauritius a number of Coolies whose time had expired. When she left Calcutta to go to the Mauritius with 210 Coolies (the full number permitted), she only lost three of them, including a woman, who died in child-birth. When she returned, she brought 270 Coolies—nearly a third more than her permitted number—and of these she lost seventeen. To the fact that so much more than the proper number was carried, do the local writers, who take the humane view of the question, attribute the increase of mortality, and the melancholy event gives them an opportunity of contrasting the conduct of the public authorities at the Mauritius with that of the authorities of Calcutta. At Calcutta, as we have seen, no more than the right number could be shipped, and there are at the same place a variety of regulations concerning the supply of provisions for the voyage. At the Mauritius, on the contrary, no such regulations seem to exist, or *if they do exist, they are completely inoperative;* and the assertion is well borne out, that after the engagement of the Coolies has expired, all concern for their

Hindoo entrapped into such a community, unacquainted with their language, without money, and unable to return to his own country for five years, (save at an expense, under the most fortunate circumstances, of forty rupees,) can hardly be the subject of favourable anticipations; and when it is taken into consideration that under the circumstances into which the immigrant is thrown, the sanctity of his peculiar religious views is unavoidably broken through, while at the same time the presence and exertions of Christian Missionaries are understood to have been discouraged as tending to render him restless and dissatisfied, it will not be matter of wonder that in one of the despatches from Sir Lionel Smith, the Governor, it is stated, that " the Coolies already introduced had given themselves up to a degree of disgraceful licentiousness which no person acquainted with their character and habits in India (dissolute as they are known to be) could possibly believe." *

welfare ceases. There appears to be no necessity for providing medicine or medical attendance, and all that the captain is bound to furnish is a pound and a half of rice daily, two pounds of salt fish per week (which is found positively injurious), and some salt and wood, with accommodations for cooking. No regard is paid to the number of Coolies put on board, and the owners may cram their vessels as much as they think fit. Thus, while every precaution is taken on the voyage from India to the Mauritius through the humane exertions of the Bengal authorities, the very reverse is the case on the voyage back. The Government of India is totally powerless in this matter, and the local writers urgently call for the interference of the home Government. In two ships, it seems, no less than sixty-one persons have perished.

* It is curious that, in the face of this, Sir Lionel Smith has no

The extent of the frauds by which these immigrations were effected can hardly be conceived; yet it is quite evident that so long as immigration continues it can only be by similar means. In support of the assertion that " in the absence of fraud no labourer from among the Coolie race could be induced to leave his country," a significant fact was mentioned a year or two back in the House of Commons. It was stated that a Mr. Dowson, who had himself been engaged in exporting Indian labourers to the Mauritius, became so convinced of the fraudulent system by which the Coolies were entrapped, that he determined not to employ the crimps and duffadars to procure them, but to send a special agent. " My orders," he said, " were to engage no Coolie without first explaining to him the nature of the employment, and that he was to leave his country for a period of five years." It proved a fruitless mission, for he did not succeed in procuring a single Coolie, and that at the very time that duffadars sent by another party were engaging Coolies by hundreds in the immediate vicinity. On the possibility of

hesitation in asserting that "although he will not promise that no injustice or oppression shall be practised towards those who may hereafter emigrate, they will be infinitely better off than in their own overstocked country, and that their mercenary habits will be gratified to the ultimate advantage of India and Mauritius." The bettering process appears from this view to consist in drawing a man from his home, family, and friends, in order to gratify his " mercenary habits,"—even though such gratification may lead to a " disgraceful licentiousness" previously unknown.

arranging a system by which fraud might be prevented, Lord Auckland, as Governor-General of India, gave his opinion:—" I greatly fear that though amendment and caution would no doubt come with time, no strictness of regulation, no vigilance on the part of the authorities, would immediately prevent the frequent infliction of grievous oppressions and deceits upon large numbers of persons, helpless from their poverty and from their utter ignorance and inexperience."

It is impossible to convey to the ignorant Coolie any idea of the nature of the engagement into which he enters when he consents to emigrate. He knows nothing of geography, nothing of the sea, nothing of the effects of separation from home; and although these things may be represented to him in due form, the representation will make little impression, especially while it is sedulously coupled with appeals to those " mercenary habits" which form the worst and most active feature of his character, and which it is the duty of his fellow men to endeavour to repress. If it can be shown that the Coolie, when his ignorance is removed, is willing to serve in a foreign country, and to undertake an agreement after experience has rendered him competent to do so, there can be no objection to permission being granted; but there is but one way in which this experience can be conveyed to him. If he really understands the nature of a sea voyage and foreign labour at the time of consenting to emigrate, he will of course not wish to withdraw that consent when he finds that his views are confirmed. It would be very safe, therefore, for the Government, if they felt sure that he had not been imposed upon, to adopt any method by which this fact might be tested and the doubts of their opponents effectually removed. They might, for instance, instruct the commander of each immigrant ship, after having been two days at sea, to call all the passengers before him, to acquaint them that the passage, of which they had now had forty-eight hours' experience, would last for many weeks, and that they had then the option of continuing or returning. If no deceit had been practised, they would of course proceed; and thus, as far as the sea voyage was concerned, it would be evident they acted of their own free will. Again, as it might still happen that they had been grossly deceived regarding the nature of their destination and the work required of them, they might have an opportunity, say for three months after their arrival, of testing the lure which had been held out to them, and then of returning if they found that they had been misled. So far, however, are those who tempt the Coolie by the " infinite advantages " of emigration from being disposed to rely upon his satisfaction at these advantages when he comes to have experience of them, that a method the very opposite of this is considered necessary. Once on board ship, and bound for the West Indies, he has no opportunity of escape for five years; unless, indeed, at the end of a less time he may have succeeded in accumulating 12*l.* sterling, and should be willing to sacrifice it to purchase his deliverance.

In a measure of emancipation, then, the defects of which has led to the adoption of remedies such as these, we can find nothing but what is to be shunned; and even if the method above stated were adopted so as to prevent the Coolie immigration from being what it now is—a new form of slavery, although one gross feature of injustice would be removed, the disastrous clumsiness of the whole would still stand forth. When we see the planters openly denied the full compensation admitted to be their due, the produce of the colonies reduced nearly one half, the coloured race perilled by habits of luxurious indolence, the slave-trade stimulated, and the prejudices of slave-holding countries confirmed, we almost come to the conclusion that further mischief is impossible; but when we are told that, in consequence of these things, a permanent protection is to be granted to the planters out of the pockets of the poor of England—that an immigration is to take place of thousands of labourers (to restore the country under freedom to its prosperity under slavery), at an expense for each, for five years only, of 24*l.* sterling—and that an influx is to be permitted amongst the coloured population of a new race, notoriously " dissolute," and prone to " disgraceful licentiousness," we learn that the evil may yet by one means be increased, and that this means is to be found in the adoption of " remedies" suggested by those who continue the disregard of principle in which alone it had its origin.

In closing this section, it is necessary to touch upon an experiment in connexion with the slave question, which has been widely promoted for nearly thirty years,—that of the American Colonization Society, for shipping off to their settlement of Liberia the free people of colour residing in the United States. Whether this scheme, however, has any bearing on emancipation so as to bring it strictly within the scope of our inquiries, it is somewhat difficult to ascertain; its promoters having occasionally described it as comprehending " the only possible mode of emancipation, at once safe and rational, that human ingenuity can devise," and at other times, as " disclaiming all intention whatever of interfering in the smallest degree with the rights of property or the object of emancipation, gradual or immediate."

The total receipts of this society are alleged to have amounted to 300,000 or 400,000 dollars; and I find, by a recent New York journal, that "the colony of Liberia now numbers 2,463 persons, of whom 645 were born in Africa." From this statement, taking into consideration that there are 386,348 free negroes in the United States, and 2,487,355 slaves, and that the turn of the slaves for removal is not likely to come till the free blacks are got rid of, the Society certainly does not seem to call for notice as an instrument of emancipation.

The practices by which even the above limited results have been obtained are such also as to confirm this conclusion. " If the free people of colour," said the *Southern Religious Telegraph* of the 19th of February, 1831, " were generally taught to read, it might be an inducement for them to remain in this country; we would offer them no such inducement." A scheme which involves the keeping of nearly 400,000 persons in total ignorance, with the view to bring about a state of misery and degradation that may drive them in desperation from their homes, and which is persisted in, though the emigration of less than one per cent. of the population thus debased has been its sole encouragement during thirty years, can hardly be shaken in the minds of its supporters by any appeal to reason or morality. They must have reached that last stage of infatuation, to which disaster, and not warning, must supply the cure.*

Dismissing, however, all consideration of the failure

---

* " It appears questionable whether Liberia will ever raise food sufficient for a very moderate population ; and it certainly never can export any quantity of tropical produce. During the time we remained in the river St. Paul, our vessels were crowded by respectable and intelligent mulattoes, all of whom, with the exception of the coloured editor of the *Liberia Gazette*, and one or two others in the pay of the Society by whom they are sent from America, complained bitterly of the deceit that had been practised towards them, and of the privations under which they were then suffering. An intelligent mulatto said to me, on my questioning him on the subject, ' It was not exactly kidnapping, but we were inveigled away under false pretences.'

" As to civilizing Africa by means of Liberia, it is well known, that from the time the colony was first established it was constantly at war with the natives until their partial extermination left the strangers in peaceable possession."—*Laird's Expedition*.

of this Society, it seems inexplicable that at its first formation any one should have been found to regard it in the slightest degree as an aid to emancipation. The getting rid of the free blacks would render slavery more safe, and slaves more valuable; and that men who now refuse to recognize the sinfulness of the institution would, under such circumstances of increased temptation, manifest a better disposition, is hardly to be expected. "Without slaves the plantations would be worthless, — there are no white men to cultivate them," is one ground of protest against the views of the abolitionists; the destruction of the rights of property and the ruin of the proprietors, if freedom were granted without compensation, being another; both of which must be admitted valueless, if the scheme of the planters, voluntarily, and at a great expense, to ship away these cultivators and their own "right of property" at the same time, is to be received in good faith. The present value of the slave population is sometimes estimated at two or three hundred millions sterling; and the supposition that there is an intention of sacrificing this amount, either at the shrine of prejudice or principle, is not warranted by any self-denying horror of slavery or of the coloured race hitherto manifested by the Southern States.

But it will be urged that those who advocated the Liberia scheme as an instrument of emancipation, did so with the understanding that its effects would be gradual, and that it would take "at least" a hundred years to accomplish its object. Such was certainly the case, and this gives us an additional reason for dismissing it from our consideration. The scheme of sinners to insure that the advantages of sin shall be enjoyed by themselves and denied to those who may come after them, cannot present much that is instructive. When the present race are called to their account, we may believe their best plea will be found in having sought virtue while it was yet permitted them, and not in having directed their efforts to an end, which has already been made known to us as fore-ordained of Heaven, that their sins shall be repented of by a third and fourth generation.

Having arrived at the conclusion that in seeking the repression of slavery we can derive no help from precedent, we must now enter upon the question with minds as free as if it had never been the subject of legislation. In taking this step our only course is to recognize boldly the duties it involves—duties which were sought to be defined in the first section of these remarks—and to see if, by strictly attempting to fulfil them, we cannot render our task more easy than if we were to adopt the politician's plan, and to content ourselves with expedients by which they might be evaded.

SECTION III.

OF THE MEANS BY WHICH EMANCIPATION SHOULD BE EFFECTED.

IN looking at the points for which, in abolishing slavery, it is essential to provide, viz. the compensation of the planter—the permanent productiveness of the State—and the welfare of the coloured race, we observe the simple fact that the accomplishment of the whole would at once be within our power, if we could fasten upon some method by which the industry of the negro in a state of freedom could be prevented from falling below what he yields in slavery, at the same time that the rate of remuneration should be such as is paid under natural circumstances for labour of an analogous kind in other parts of the world. If this object could be attained, the source whence the means of compensation to the planter for the loss of his exclusive title to the labour of the slave is to be derived would immediately become apparent; and the mere practical arrangement by which such compensation should be conveyed to him would alone remain to be considered, because, as no diminution of labour would take place, it would be impossible for the slave-owner to be deprived of any portion of it without some one else reaping the advantage, and there would, therefore, be nothing to do but to adjust the balance between them; so that the loss sustained by one party from the labour-market being thrown open, might be made up by the other, who had taken the opportunity to come into it. The substitution of wages for the present cost of supporting the slave, supposing them to be at the same rate as is usually given for unskilled labour, would not act as a disturbing cause, since the slave never performs above half the work of a free man; and for this occupation a rate of wages that would supply him with all he now gets, viz., food, clothing, lodging, medical attendance, maintenance in old age, &c., would be more than equal to what is usually attained in free communities; few instances being known of a peasantry who, simply by working each other day, are able to insure these necessaries.*

Our chief object, then, must be to ascertain if there is any mode consistent with justice by which the natural powers of the negro may thus be developed so as to induce on his part an obedience to the great condition of all human progress—that each man shall exert such faculties as may have been bestowed upon him to the fullest extent that is consistent with the happiness of others.

It will hardly be contended that the faculties of the negro in his present stage can be beneficially deve-

---

* "In the laborious occupation of holing, the emancipated negroes perform double the work of a slave in a day. In road-making the day's task, under slavery, was to break four barrels of stone. *Now*, by task-work, a weak hand will fill eight barrels, a strong one from ten to twelve barrels."—*Gurney*.

loped in any other way than by the rudest occupations of agriculture or art, and it is therefore by constant diligence in this direction that he best fulfils the duties of his being. It is true he is capable of warm domestic feelings; but the proper action of these, so far from being inconsistent with healthy industry, would render it light and cheerful. Now the exercise of these powers of usefulness which he possesses can only be drawn from him as it is drawn from others, by acting in some way upon his predominant desires. In a high state of civilization all the faculties of the mind are more or less in exercise, and everything in nature, therefore, stirs us to activity; but in a lower stage the lower faculties are alone powerful, and the means of suggesting motives to exertion are consequently very limited. That they are not so limited, however, in the present instance as to be inadequate to the desired end, we have sufficient reason to believe; because we have seen that even the slave-trader and slave-owner, acting in all the ignorance of selfish depravity, have been able in their blind way to achieve the object of compelling the negro to work; and it would be monstrous to suppose that a success which has been attained by such minds is beyond the reach of that wisdom which seeks its ends only by virtuous means; that the short-sighted cunning, in fact, of predominant propensities can grasp even temporarily what the harmonious action of reason and morality would attempt in vain.

In considering the negro in his present stage of mental development, we perceive manifestations of strong sensual appetites, intense domestic attachments, cautiousness, love of money, vanity, and a disposition to reverence. These then are the chief materials presented for us to work upon in endeavouring to lead him to useful ends ; the remaining mental faculties being rarely, either singly or combined, so eager for gratification as to impel him to attain it by self-denial in other respects. But while we see that the gratification of the lower faculties which I have named would present the only inducement that would stimulate him to exertion, we are required to bear in mind, that as they are already predominant, his advancement can only be aided by calling into play those which are at present inactive; so as to bring the various powers of the mind to that harmonious and active state to which they approach among more civilized races. This being the case, it must be improper to hold out as a bait any additional gratification of the inferior faculties, and hence a difficulty arises; since, if we are forbidden to stimulate the only desires which are strong enough to act as inducements, it is not at first sight easy to discover by what means we are to operate upon him at all. "It may be very well," it will be said, "to appeal to intellect, benevolence, conscience, taste, and all the finer powers, and to show how he might gratify them by the produce of his labour; but until by long training these powers have been rendered active, we shall only appeal to them in vain. There is no present chance, then, of arousing him by this means; and yet we are told that the remaining faculties are to be repressed rather than excited. What in such case is to be done? If we could hold out to him as the reward of labour some new indulgences of his sensual desires, some enormous increase of wages, or some undue gratification of vanity,—or even if we might stimulate his already over-developed sense of fear by a recourse to personal inflictions, it is easy to see that more work might be obtained; but while these stimulants are denied, and it is admitted that there are no others that would prove effectual, it seems hard to comprehend that any means exist by which our object may be effected."

But the difficulty, though great, is not insurmountable. Although his predominant propensities already find sufficient gratification, and must not be further encouraged, it remains for us to inquire if there is not some portion of this gratification the just enjoyment of which is inconsistent with a neglect of industry, and if so, whether it is not possible as a consequence of such neglect to enforce a *deprivation* of what is now permitted to him?

There can be no doubt that if we were to deny him the enjoyment of eating or drinking until he consented to work, or if we were to separate him from his wife and children, permitting him to join them only on the same conditions, or if we could induce all his fellows to regard idleness as a disgrace, and to refuse to associate with him until he became industrious, we should accomplish our end; but none of these means are open to us, since the former would be an outrage on his liberty, and the latter is an impossibility. By taking food, and by enjoying the society of his wife and children, he merely gratifies natural faculties without in any way interfering with the happiness of others.

One of the strongest propensities of his nature, however, and intimately connected with his other domestic impulses, is his attachment to home or country. This feeling, innate in all men, has long been observed to display itself with singular force in the character of the negro. Amongst all races there exists to a greater or less degree a blind attachment to the place they have long inhabited, apart from the mere effect of association, which can never be entirely overcome, and which has evidently been implanted by the Creator for the wisest purposes. To man, in a rude stage of society, it seems especially essential, since as the first step towards founding communities, or the pursuit of agriculture, it is necessary for him to adopt a permanent location; a necessity to which he is adapted, and the fulfilment of which is rendered agreeable to him by the existence of this faculty. In many of the lower animals the same propensity is to be remarked, "Migratory animals," it has been observed, "return thousands of miles to reach the same spot that they inhabited the year before. In doing this, they have no apparent motive but attachment to the place. It cannot be to find food, for they often pass other locations which are superior in this respect to their own homes; nor can it be attachment to their former companions, for they go with them and return with them. In many instances they not only return to the same country, but to the same tree or bank, or house, and even to the same nest. The propensity seems also powerfully developed in the cat, who will leave all her old friends, and taking her kittens in her mouth, return several miles to her accustomed residence." That this propensity exists in man, as well as in the lower animals, irrespective of the effects of reason or association, is shown by the fact that it is usually strongest in the least cultivated minds, while if it were a consequence of the increased powers of association which high training brings, it would of course be found to increase in force with the progress of civilization. So far from this being the case, we have evidence of the feeling being manifested in the most intense form by the most barbarous races; cases of death from nostalgia, the peculiar disease caused by its morbid action, having been reported even amongst the aborigines of Van Dieman's Land. It is from its activity, too, that much of the repugnance to emigration amongst the lower classes of society which is shown under the severest pressure, and where the opportunity is afforded them of taking their entire families, and of accompanying their friends, is to be accounted for;

whilst we may also attribute to it, in some degree, the salutary effect which the dread of perpetual banishment is found to produce on the most depraved.

But whether it be regarded as arising from a primary faculty of the mind, or merely as the result of association, the fact is unquestionable, that the emotion itself is common to human nature, and, especially, that it exercises an imperative sway over the negro race.

In the evidence given before a Committee of the British Parliament, it was shown that the slaves in the West Indies had a great objection to being removed even from one estate to another in the same island. Indeed, it was stated by one or two witnesses that when it was proposed to remove them from an unhealthy situation to a better one they declined the offer. In Jamaica, after emancipation, the planters, knowing the strength of this feeling, resorted to threats of ejectment to compel labour; and so tenacious were the negroes of their immediate homesteads, that cottages have been unroofed, and even demolished, cocoa-nut and bread-fruit trees have been cut down, and provision grounds despoiled, before they could be driven to move away to other properties. In some instances, the plan of doubling or trebling the rent, or even multiplying it fourfold, or charging it *per capita* against husband, wife, and each of the children, seems to have failed to drive them away. In an instance of the removal of slaves from the Bahamas to Trinidad, they are stated all to have " pined away;" and Sir Fowell Buxton, in contending against permission being given to remove the coloured apprentices from one colony to another, alluded in the House of Commons to similar cases. " The late Mr. Maryat," he said, " stated in this house, in my hearing, that the negroes died off when they came to Trinidad like 'rotten sheep.' Sir John Cotton hesitated not to say that it would have been less cruel to have shot them through the head than to have so transported them. A case was tried in this country respecting a claim for some slaves removed from Tobago to Trinidad. The person who received them refused to pay the demand made upon him; and he distinctly proved that the whole body of negroes—men, women, and children—died within two years after they arrived at Trinidad. My firm conviction is, that if you were to permit their removal, more than twenty thousand would be removed in the course of seven or eight years from island to island, and that not one in twenty would be alive at the end of their apprenticeship. In the case of the removal of some slaves from Tobago to Trinidad, we were told that the negroes were most anxious to be removed; the next thing we heard of was an insurrection; and the last account was, that they were taken, put in irons, and re-transported from Trinidad to Tobago." Sir Fowell Buxton also quotes Mr. Young as an authority on negro character, who says that they are as much attached to the estate on which they have lived for years as the peasantry are described to be in the "Deserted Village." "Of all beings in the world," said Mr. P. M. Stewart, an advocate of the West India interests, "those most attached to localities are the negroes."

In the state of Virginia, when the original bill for an appropriation to the Colonization Society was under discussion, a Mr. Brodnax is reported to have observed, in relation to a clause for the compulsory transportation of free blacks, "It is my opinion that few, very few, will voluntarily consent to emigrate, if no compulsory measures be adopted. Without it, you will still, no doubt, have applicants for removal —people who will not only consent, but beg you to deport them. But what sort of consent?—a consent extorted by a species of oppression, calculated to render their situation among us insupportable!" To which another member, Mr. Fisher, added, "If we wait till the free negroes *consent* to leave the State, we shall wait till time is no more. They never will give their consent."

The best informed writers also allude to the same peculiarity. Mr. Gurney speaks of them as "fondly attached to their humble homes," and alludes to the strength with which this feeling sways them, (whether they be "educated or uneducated,") to account for the fact that, in the island of Dominica they prefer remaining to labour in the old districts, instead of giving way to the temptation of squatting in idleness on the wild lands. Describing the Antilles, and the constant convulsions by which they are devastated, it is remarked by Mr. Breen, in his work just published on St. Lucia, " The fact is, between fires and hurricanes and earthquakes, the bewildered inhabitant of these islands scarcely knows where to go or what to do; and yet with all their disadvantages and dangers, he still fondly clings to the wild western rocks of his birth." Mr. Featherstonhaugh relates that Mr. Madison, the Ex-president, once informed him that he had assembled all his slaves,—and they were numerous,— and offered to manumit them immediately, but that they instantly declined it, alleging, amongst other reasons, that they had been *born* on his estate, and that if they were made free they would have no home to go to. Mr. Burnley, of Trinidad, by whom more than ordinary opportunities were possessed of observing the negro character, says, "The African is found to be naturally attached to the spot which he inhabits. Even the peon who migrates annually from the adjoining continent to labour in Trinidad, regularly returns when the crop is over to his accustomed home." This kind of attachment is no less observable even in the midst of his original barbarism. " The great object of the krooman, or the fishman (the most prone to emigration of all the negro race) is to get," says Mr. Laird, " the means of purchasing as many wives as will keep him in idleness in his own country."

Now the gratification of this propensity—this love of home—involves, as does also the gratification of every other desire, a necessity for the fulfilment of certain coincident duties. The indulgence, for instance, of the affection which leads to the union of the sexes, imposes the responsibility of faithfully maintaining the partner selected; and if this is not fulfilled, steps are taken to enforce it. The enjoyment of parental love in like manner brings with it the obligation to attend to the physical and moral improvement of the offspring, and when such obligation is neglected, it becomes proper for the State to fulfil the task, and to deny the offenders the presence of their children. The same may be said of all human feelings; they have all their legitimate sphere of action, as also their inseparable duties. The love of home forms no exception to this rule. The soil to which we attach ourselves has capabilities of rendering gifts which would minister not only to our own advancement but also to the happiness of our fellows. We have no title to sit down upon it in sloth; the penalty of a disregard of the laws of the Creator must inevitably follow such a course; and it is the duty of a government to avert this consequence by rendering the gratification of the propensity dependent on the strict fulfilment of the duties which it involves.

The position of the negro, and the way in which in his case this doctrine is to be applied, is very simple. He has been unjustly brought into the condition he now occupies through violence perpetrated either upon himself or his progenitors, and he has consequently an incontestable right to demand at any time to be restored to the state whence he was so iniquitously removed. No social laws, therefore, can properly be enforced against him until the best atonement within reach has been offered for this original sin, and which must consist in giving him the option of living in that country which he is entitled to consider his own, and where he would now have existed but for our misdeeds. When this offer has been made, and the acceptance of it refused, he becomes at once and for the first time a voluntary member of our community, and, of course, bound to submit to every law which we may adopt; it being at the same time incumbent on the Government that such laws shall be entirely consistent with the enjoyment on his part of life, liberty, and the pursuit of happiness.

The plain course of duty, then, is at once to set him free, and to give him the option of a passage to Africa; intimating to him that if he prefers to remain where he is, so far from being permitted to live in idleness or in the habitual indulgence of any other vice, such laws will be adopted with regard to him as may seem best calculated to promote his own advancement and his general usefulness to society. Upon the condition of obedience to these laws the consent on the part of the Government to his remaining should distinctly depend, and banishment should consequently be the penalty for their infringement.

Now, after what is known of the intense attachment

of the negro to his accustomed home, no matter on what continent that home may be,—after the ineffectual efforts that have been witnessed both in the British possessions and in America, by means of bribery, fraud, and persecution, to induce him, when it has been needed, to quit the soil to which he has become attached, it cannot be believed for one moment that if set free in the United States he would select transportation to Africa rather than consent to the condition of continuing an amount of labour equal to that which he had executed during slavery,—an amount which, in a state of liberty, would be less than half of what he might with ease perform. Let this condition, therefore, be enforced, and all danger of the negro becoming less useful in freedom than in slavery would be at once removed.*

By a step of this kind, then, it is in the power of the United States to comply at once with that point of the moral law which requires that no parley should be held with sin. They have only to recognize the iniquity of slave-holding, and they may cast it off to-morrow. A little examination will show that by the plan now stated, not only would the great

* In some of the older West India islands, where the coloured population is comparatively dense, the negroes, in order to obtain subsistence, find it necessary to perform an amount of work equal to their work as slaves. Yet, although instead of the alternative of a voyage to Africa, they have the power of merely removing to a neighbouring island, in order, by a tenth part of the labour, to attain the same profit, they are not only contented, but for the most part desirous to remain.

objects of maintaining the prosperity of the country and the progress of the negro be accomplished, but —such is the harmony of just and natural legislation —it would also, in its practical arrangements, present full means, to the minutest fraction, of affording compensation to the proprietors.

And first, as to the practical part of the plan, so far as it is to provide for the enforcement of continued industry. It is of course to be understood that the negro is to be set entirely at liberty, with the world before him where to choose his dwelling-place; nay, more, that he should have the option of a free passage to Africa, so soon as arrangements could be made to that effect. But if, as assuredly would be the case, he should cling to his present home in preference to Africa, it must be an imperative condition of his remaining in the United States that he shall pursue such a course as will prove consistent with his own happiness and the general happiness of the people; that amongst an industrious race, actively using their various talents, it shall not be a permission to him alone to live in open disregard of the duty of contributing by the best exercise of his powers to the common weal. To gain the privilege of remaining he will, of course, accede to the condition; but his promise would soon be broken, unless means could be taken constantly to enforce it. To effect this, imprisonment would obviously be useless, and personal inflictions would be still more objectionable; the former would be disregarded by the indolent, and the latter would only debase and harden both the sufferer and his judge, while each alike would prove more or less inconsistent with the Christian code. Indolence is a peculiarity of his race, and if those amongst whom he desires to live cannot overcome this peculiarity by just and humane treatment, all that they are entitled to do is to forbid him to remain, and to banish him to the country in which alone he can rightfully claim a residence. This penalty, therefore, is the only one that can legitimately be used; but as it has been found in all countries to be the most severe, and such as, in the case of the negro, would be more terrible than death itself, it would prove amply sufficient for its object. It should, therefore, constantly be kept before his eyes as the immediate consequence of disobedience.

Towards this end a general registration of the coloured population should be effected, and an amount of labour equal to the average labour of a slave should be fixed as the daily "task" of each. At the end of every three or six months the negro should be required to deliver or to transmit to an officer, appointed by the Government for that purpose, a certificate or certificates from the employer whom he may have served, of his having performed the required amount of labour (of course bodily infirmity would prove an exemption) during the specified period; failing in which, he should be declared liable to deportation. Further details as to any grace which might be allowed after such failure, when the full consequences of his course were presented to him, and when he might desire an opportunity of amendment, need not be considered here : he might perhaps be permitted in a second three months to make up the defalcation in the first, or he might be received on probation at some Government depôt, and allowed an opportunity, by employment at road-making, or in some other manner, of working the required time and averting his sentence. Forbearance of this kind, however, should have well-defined limits, and, as an example to others, a second offence should be followed by his immediate departure.

But although it will be seen that by this means the industry of the country will be kept up to its present amount, we must be careful to avoid a fallacy which found a prominent place in the debates of the British Parliament, viz.: that if you do not take away the labourer from the soil, his former proprietor can have no claim for compensation for the loss of his services. It is true, when the supply of labour remains the same, if the slaves upon emancipation quit their master, he can easily supply their place by others, and at a rate of wages not exceeding his previous outlay; but, under these circumstances, what takes place? During the old system, in order to cultivate an estate an outlay of capital was required to purchase the requisite number of hands, and this outlay was, of course, so much to be taken off the value of the land. If a certain number of acres required an outlay of 1000 dollars to render them profitable, a person in purchasing those acres would not give so much for them by 1000 dollars as he would give if no such outlay was necessary. If, therefore, you set the negroes free, and upon terms which shall not raise their wages beyond the cost of maintaining slaves, you increase the value of each estate by just so much as it would have taken to stock it with a sufficient supply of labourers. In Antigua, where, owing to the comparative density of the population, the price of labour is not raised above its cost in slavery, Sir William Colebrooke, the Governor-General, informed Mr. Gurney that "at the lowest computation, the land, without a single slave upon it, is fully as valuable now as it was, including all the slaves, before emancipation.

Now, if every slave-owner were a land-owner to a proportionate extent, this might cause no injury, because the rise in the value of the one would compensate for the loss of the capital laid out on the other; but, as this is not the case,—many persons holding slaves without an acre of land, while others hold land without slaves,—a manifest injustice would arise. The increased value of the land would be caused solely by the presence of available labourers, the procuring and raising of whom had been entirely effected by the capital of the slave-owner; and, as this additional value would precisely amount to the market price of what is at present looked upon as his property, it is clear that out of his pocket would come every dollar that the land-owner might gain.

In order to prevent this, and to avert all disturbance of the present relations of capital, a very obvious plan presents itself. Let each person granting certificates of the employment of negroes be required to use annually for each a Government stamp, say, for example, to the amount of thirty-two dollars, and to each proprietor of a slave at the date of emancipation let there be given a deed of exemption (to be called a compensation deed) from the use of such stamp. Estimating the value of a slave at 500 dollars, the yearly interest upon this at 6 per cent. would amount to thirty dollars; and in order that the marketable nature of his slave property might still attach to the "compensation deed," by which it is represented, the holder should have the power of transferring his right of exemption either temporarily or permanently to others. As no one would be able to employ a negro without paying thirty-two dollars per annum, or the possession of one of these deeds, the annual market value of the privilege they convey could never, under any natural circumstances, fall below thirty or thirty-one dollars, because it would always be desirable for an employer to purchase at that price exemption from the stamp, and consequently the market value of the deed itself would stand at 500 dollars. By this arrangement, therefore, the proprietor would receive full compensation, and the price of land would remain undisturbed, — since each person buying an estate would reckon as at present, that it would cost him 500 dollars, or the annual interest of that sum for every labourer whom he might employ to work it.*

* Of course, in carrying out this plan, it would be essential not

The final absorption of the compensation deeds thus created would take place at no distant day; as the negroes, by the influence of a well-regulated freedom, gradually attained to respectability and competence, certificates would be purchased by individuals amongst them desirous of getting rid of the necessity of specified labour. Such purchases would be analogous to any other investment, and would, in fact, supposing the compensation due to the proprietor had been transferred, as in Antigua, to the land, be the same as if they had purchased so much real estate. The annual income derivable from such estate will be represented by the artificial increase to the value of their labour, if they choose to work ; and in the event of their living upon their savings, it will be represented by the exemption from that taxation which property must have borne if they had been suffered to live in idleness on any other terms.*

to lose sight of the difference of value arising from sex, age, &c.; but as no difficulty would arise from this circumstance, it is enough, in this place, to indicate the general principle.

To promote the convenience of the holders, the deeds of exemption might be transferable with quarterly or half-yearly coupons attached, which could be forwarded to the Government offices along with the labour certificates, in lieu of the stamp they must otherwise bear. Supposing the holder had not employed any labour during the period, he would of course dispose of them in the market to those who had.

* These regulations regarding labour should also apply to the coloured population already free; but, as in selling, or in voluntarily granting emancipation, their owners gave up to them the amount which, under a system for the due maintenance of industry, would

It may appear to some, at first sight, that if the above plan were carried out, although the supply of labour would remain the same, the rate of wages would rise, owing to the efforts of the planters to outbid one another. But this is impossible. In purchasing their estates, in expending money on them, and in paying for their negroes, the planters gave a price which, after calculating the cost of slave maintenance, would afford them just a reasonable profit, compared with the profit to be derived from other investments. In order to continue this profit, then, it is out of the question that they can afford to pay more in the shape of wages, because they could get no return for such additional payment. The increase of wages in the West Indies was made up by the rise in the price of produce ; but no such rise could take place in the United States, because the price depends entirely on the supply, and the supply would not be lessened as it was in the British colonies. If therefore one planter should outbid another in the rate of wages for the sake of obtaining a larger share of negro labour, (offering more for the "tasks" of the negroes than is at present paid for them in the shape of food, clothing, &c.,) he would cease to derive a remunerating profit, and must soon run into insolvency.

then have been transferred to the land, it would be proper that the stamp duty accruing from this source should be applied solely for their benefit ;—in the establishment, for instance, of educational, religious, or other institutions, as might be deemed advisable.

It is plain from the foregoing considerations that it is in the power of the United States to turn from the sin of slavery, not only without even temporary damage to any worldly interest, but with the assurance of an increased prosperity. The half-time labour (for it would not amount to more) of the free coloured population would soon be voluntarily extended, and by every hour so gained the wealth of the country and the value of its soil would be proportionably increased.

Before dismissing these suggestions, I must not omit to mention a difficulty—the only one present to my mind—which, although slight in its nature, might be alleged as likely to interfere with their success. Those who may be disposed to concede at once the utter improbability of the American negro preferring transportation to Africa, to comfort, protection, and freedom in his native land, will still, perhaps, point to the West Indies, and remind us that although he may, in the first instance, be landed in Africa, he would soon find that he had it in his power to quit that continent for the British colonies; that his passage would be eagerly provided by active agents, and that representations would be industriously made to him of the luxurious indolence which he would there be permitted to enjoy. I do not believe that these representations would have the effect desired, because we have already seen that the negroes will not purchase exemption from toil at a cost of a sacrifice of home, even when the removal is only to a neighbouring colony; but it is, nevertheless, desirable that their influence should be prevented. To this end it may be assumed that the British Government (supposing them unable to devise means of bringing their colonies to a healthy condition) would readily undertake to prohibit the introduction into these possessions of immigrants transported to Africa from the United States. Despite the defective plans of their statesmen, it cannot be doubted that the people of England are sincere in their abhorrence of slavery ; and we may therefore fairly hope that they are not destined to the humiliation of finding that, instead of being the leaders of emancipation, they form the only impediment to its course.

To conclude. It will perhaps be asked by those who have paid attention to the general tenor of my views, if there is not, some contradiction to the doctrine maintained in them throughout—that sin is invariably the parent of disaster — in a plan which claims to abolish slavery in the United States without inflicting the slightest suffering ; and if it is not dangerous to assert that a crime so grievous can be suddenly cast off, and, with it, all apprehension of the judgments of the Creator ? I reply, that those judgments have already fallen, and that the immediate effect of a sincere repentance will be, not to wipe out the penalties thus far incurred, but to avert those which must, with every day's continuance of evil, inevitably accumulate, — penalties which, although unseen in their approach, are foreknown by those who trust in the justice of Heaven, and are not less present to them as things that must be, when the wrong-doer stands boastingly in the glare of success, than when the threatenings of his failing fortunes may be distinctly heard. In the degrading terror avowed at the consequences of granting freedom to the negro—in the self-condemning caution with which the approach of knowledge, the common foe of tyrants, is barred from his mind—in the impatience of contradiction which, even among equals, renders the bowie-knife an argument—in the absence of steady enterprise and provident cultivation—in the misgivings which, amidst every boast of national power, tell of three millions of enemies,—enemies that might have been friends, clustered on the soil—and in that wilful deadening of the moral sense which, manifested first in a denial of the primary right of humanity, ends in a reckless repudiation of every other claim, the penalties of slavery past and present are sufficiently unfolded. When to these we add that the "Union," which might have formed a type of the eventual brotherhood of nations, is rendered insecure and soulless; that in its legislative halls even the right of petition is denied, and that LIBERTY, as she dwells in the land of Washington, is made a bye-word and a jest to distant regions of the earth, the conviction rises that the future can have little more of warning to impart, and that if America—reckless that the responsibility and peril of sin increases with the light bestowed—continues to cling, amidst the spreading radiance of Christianity, to the darkest barbarism that ever disgraced the world, the hour of her severest doom must rapidly approach. That this doom may be averted, and that she may yet gain the course to which she once seemed destined, will be the earnest prayer of all who faithfully seek the advancement of mankind.

NOTE.

"THE RIGHT OF PETITION."

SINCE the date of the foregoing letter the rule of Congress prohibiting the reception of petitions against Slavery has been rescinded. "We think," says the *New York Courier and Enquirer* of the 7th of December last, "every person who appreciates the real character of the liberty we enjoy must be heartily gratified at the success at last achieved by John Quincy Adams, in his long-continued efforts to procure the rescinding of the disgraceful rule which has heretofore excluded a certain class of petitions from the floor of Congress. The right to petition is certainly one of which no citizen should ever be deprived, and we sincerely rejoice that the representatives of the people have at last concluded to hear, with at least a show of respect, the petitions of those by whom they are chosen, and from whom they derive all the power they possess. We trust now that these petitions on the subject of Slavery will be received, read, and referred to an appropriate Committee like all other papers; and that the subject will be considered and presented to the country precisely as its great importance and its merits deserve."

LONDON:
Printed by S. & J. BENTLEY, WILSON, and FLEY,
Bangor House, Shoe Lane.

NEW MEDICAL WORKS,
PUBLISHED BY
SAMUEL HIGHLEY, 32, FLEET STREET,
OPPOSITE ST. DUNSTAN'S CHURCH.

TRAVERS ON INFLAMMATION.
THE PHYSIOLOGY OF INFLAMMATION AND THE HEALING PROCESS.
By BENJAMIN TRAVERS, F.R.S., Surgeon Extraordinary to the Queen, &c.
8vo. Price 7s.

"We believe that it may rank amongst the most important contributions which the literature of this department has received in modern times."—*Forbes' Medical Review.*
"We know of no treatise whatever in which these interesting processes (inflammation and the subsequent stages of reparation) are described so clearly and completely as in the work before us."—*Provincial Medical Journal.*
"The subjects discussed are of paramount importance, and the author has evidently prepared himself well for the task. The book to be understood must be carefully and diligently perused, and we strongly recommend it to every one who wishes to practise Surgery on a scientific basis."—*Edinburgh Journal of Medical Science.*

PARIS'S PHARMACOLOGIA. 9th Edit.
Being an extended inquiry into the operations of Medicinal Bodies, upon which are founded
THE THEORY AND ART OF PRESCRIBING.
Re-written, in order to incorporate the latest Discoveries in Physiology, Chemistry, and Materia Medica.
By J. A. PARIS, M.D., F.R.S., President of the Royal College of Physicians. 8vo, Price 20s.

"Dr. Paris's work contains a great mass of useful and important Pharmacological information, both theoretical and practical, on topics not discussed in other works, either British or Foreign. To it, therefore, all succeeding writers on these subjects must be indebted; and every intelligent student and practitioner must have recourse to it if they desire to be on a level with the existing condition of our knowledge of the action of medicines, and the principles and art of prescribing.
"The present edition has been entirely re-written."—*Medical Gazette.*

GUY'S HOSPITAL REPORTS, New Series.
Vol. I—1843. Price 16s. 6d. Vol. II—1844. Price 13s. cloth lettered.

It is proposed, in this Series, to devote a large portion of each Number to Reports of the most interesting Cases occurring within the Hospital, illustrated by plates. These Cases will be Classified, so as to present the History of any particular Disease, as it has occurred in the Hospital.
To be continued in half yearly parts published in April and October, Price 6s. each, and in yearly volumes.
The First Series is complete in 7 Volumes.
*** GUY'S HOSPITAL PHARMACOPŒIA, Price 4s. 6d.

JUDD ON THE VENEREAL.
A PRACTICAL TREATISE ON URETHRITIS AND SYPHILIS:
Including Observations on the power of the Menstruous Fluid, and of the Discharge from Leucorrhœa and Sores to produce Urethritis, with a variety of
EXAMPLES, EXPERIMENTS, REMEDIES AND CURES.
By WILLIAM H. JUDD, Surgeon in the Fusilier Guards. 8vo. Price 25s. with numerous coloured Plates.

BENNETT ON HYDROCEPHALUS.
An Essay on the Nature, Diagnosis, and Treatment of
ACUTE HYDROCEPHALUS,
Being the Fothergellian Prize Essay of the Medical Society of London.
By J. RISDON BENNETT, M.D. 8vo, Price 8s.

"We have perused this work with unmixed satisfaction, and congratulate the London Medical Society at having elicited so valuable a contribution from its talented author."—*Johnson's Med. Chir. Review.*
"It is a most excellent prize Essay— evidently the production of a well informed writer, and able physician."—*Forbes' Medical Review.*

HIGHLEY'S GENERAL MEDICAL CATALOGUE
Of Modern Works, with their Prices and Dates. Price 1s.
Corrected to the end of 1844.

PUBLISHED BY S. HIGHLEY, 32, FLEET STREET.

CLENDON ON EXTRACTION OF TEETH. 2nd Edit.

OBSERVATIONS ON THE EXTRACTION OF TEETH,
Being a practical Inquiry into the advantages and propriety attending the employment of properly constructed Forceps, and an Exposition of the dangers to which the use of the Key is liable.

By J. CHITTY CLENDON, Surgeon-Dentist, 2nd edit. enlarged, Price 4s. fcap. 8vo, with Plates.

"This little book, written in an excellent spirit, deserves to be examined by every person who gives advice on diseases of the teeth, or operates upon them for their removal. We have never seen a more satisfactory literary production devoted to a single subject (the extraction) from the pen of a dentist.—In the present case we have a sound practical work, evidently the result of a simple and sincere desire to be useful in the art, not hastily produced, but based on careful reflection and experience, and well meriting the best character that can be given to it by a medical journalist."—*Lancet.*

COOPER'S OSTEOLOGY.

LECTURES ON OSTEOLOGY, including the Ligaments which connect the Bones of the Human Skeleton.

By B. B. COOPER, F.R.S., Surgeon to Guy's Hospital, &c. 8vo, with Plates, Price 8s.

MORTIMER ON THE TEETH OF CHILDREN. 2nd Ed.

OBSERVATIONS on the GROWTH and IRREGULARITIES of CHILDREN'S TEETH, followed by Remarks and Advice on the Teeth in general.

By W. H. MORTIMER, late Surgeon Dentist to the British Embassy, Paris. *Just Ready.*

PILCHER ON DISEASES, &c. OF THE EAR.

A TREATISE ON THE STRUCTURE, ECONOMY, AND DISEASES OF THE EAR.
By GEORGE PILCHER, Senior Surgeon to the Surrey Dispensary.

A NEW AND IMPROVED EDITION,
In which an entirely new set of Plates is given, with additional Illustrations, 8vo, Price 12s.

"The perusal of this work has afforded us much pleasure—A work was wanted to place the whole subject within the grasp of all surgeons who choose to devote some little exclusive or particular study to the diseases of the Ear, and this has fairly and well supplied the place."—*Johnson's Med. Chir. Review.*

BELL ON DISEASES, &c. OF THE TEETH.

THE ANATOMY, PHYSIOLOGY, AND DISEASES OF THE TEETH.
By THOMAS BELL, F.R.S., F.L.S., F.G.S.,
Lecturer on Diseases of the Teeth at Guy's Hospital, and Professor of Zoology in King's College. Second Edition, 8vo, Price 14s. Containing upwards of 100 Figures, illustrative of the Structure, Growth, Diseases, &c., of the Teeth.

RAMSBOTHAM'S OBSERVATIONS IN MIDWIFERY.

PRACTICAL OBSERVATIONS IN MIDWIFERY, WITH A SELECTION OF CASES.
By JOHN RAMSBOTHAM, M.D. A New Edition, Enlarged and Revised. 1 vol. 8vo. Price 12s.

"This is an excellent work, and well deserves a place in the first rank of practical treatises on the Obstetric Art. It is pleasing to read, neither repelling us by diffuseness or tediousness, nor ever admitting of our laying down the book dissatisfied with what we may have read as an insufficient development of the subject. It is characterised throughout by the eloquence of simplicity and plain good sense, and it has the inestimable merit of keeping perpetually close to the point."—
Johnson's Med. Chir. Review.

STOWE'S CHART OF POISONS. 10th Edit.

A Toxicological Chart, exhibiting at one view the Symptoms, Treatment, and mode of Detecting the various Poisons, Mineral, Vegetable, and Animal; to which are added, Concise Directions for the Treatment of Suspended Animation.

By W. STOWE, M.R.C.S. Varnished and mounted on cloth, with roller, 6s., or 2s. the plain Sheet.

"We have placed the Chart in own Library, and we think that no medical practitioner should be without it. It should be hung up in the shops of all chemists and druggists, as well as in the dispensaries and surgeries of all general practitioners."—*Johnson's Med. Chir. Review.*

PUBLISHED BY S. HIGHLEY, 32, FLEET STREET.

MORGAN'S SURGERY.
FIRST PRINCIPLES OF SURGERY. By G. T. MORGAN. 8vo. Price 18s.

"A very excellent Treatise on Surgical Pathology, in which the author explains the leading principles of that Science with much clearness and method. The work is highly creditable not only to his talents and industry, but to his faculties of observation and reflection. With a perfect knowledge of every thing done before him, and all the illustrations furnished by the diligence of contemporary inquirers, Mr. Morgan shows very considerable originality, and great strength as well as soundness of judgment on all the topics embraced by his plan.
It may be safely recommended as an excellent treatise on the leading principles of Surgical Pathology."—
Edinburgh Medical and Surgical Journal, Jan. 1845

PHILLIPS'S PHARMACOPŒIA. 4th Edit.
A Translation of the Pharmacopœia Collegii Regalis Medicorum Londinensis, MDCCCXXXVI, with copious Notes and Illustrations; also a Table of Chemical Equivalents.

By RICHARD PHILLIPS, F.R.S., L. and E. 8vo, Price 10s. 6d.

SPRATT'S OBSTETRIC TABLES. 4th Edit.
These Tables are designed on a similar principle to Mr. Tuson's Anatomical Plates,—the Views being disposed in hinged layers, the raising of which shows a progressive advance in the subject under consideration. There are 19 Tables, most of which are made to furnish several successive views by means of this mechanical adaptation. 1 Vol. 4to, Price 28s. coloured.

INSANITY AND CRIME.
CRIMINAL JURISPRUDENCE CONSIDERED
IN RELATION TO CEREBRAL ORGANIZATION.
BY M. B. SAMPSON.
2nd Edition with considerable Additions, 8vo. Price 5s.

"We recommend this work to our readers with an assurance that they will find in it much food for reflection."—*Johnson's Med. Chir. Review.*
"Statesmen and Philanthropists, Humanity and Christianity, owe to Mr. Sampson a debt of gratitude, for having placed the question of capital punishment, and the Insanity of Criminals upon intelligible principles, which if adopted will put an end to the doubts and difficulties in which these topics have been hitherto involved, and will prepare the way for some rational and satisfactory legislation."—*Law Times.*

PROCTER ON THE SYMPATHETIC NERVE.
A TREATISE ON THE USE OF THE SYMPATHETIC NERVE AND ITS GANGLIONS, with their Influence on various Diseases of the Abdominal and Pelvic Viscera.

By T. B. PROCTER, M.D. 4to, Price 7s. 6d. with Plates.

HOCKEN'S OPHTHALMIC MEDICINE.
A COMPLETE CONDENSED PRACTICAL TREATISE ON OPHTHALMIC MEDICINE.

By E. O. HOCKEN, M.D. Fcap. 8vo, Part 1, Price 3s. To be completed in 3 parts, Price 10s. 6d.

DR. JAMES JOHNSON'S TOUR IN IRELAND,
WITH MEDITATIONS AND REFLECTIONS. 8vo, Price 8s. 6d.
BY THE SAME AUTHOR,
EXCURSIONS TO THE PRINCIPAL MINERAL WATERS OF ENGLAND, 8vo, 5s.
PILGRIMAGES TO THE GERMAN SPAS. 8vo, Price 9s.
CHANGE OF AIR, or the Pursuit of Health and Recreation. (*4th Edition*) 8vo, Price 9s.
ECONOMY OF HEALTH, or The Stream of Human Life from the Cradle to the Grave. (*4th Edition*), 8vo, Price 6s. 6d.
AN ESSAY ON INDIGESTION. (*10th Edition*) 8vo, Price 6s. 6d.
PRACTICAL RESEARCHES ON GOUT. 8vo, Price 5s. 6d.
THE INFLUENCE OF TROPICAL CLIMATES ON EUROPEAN CONSTITUTIONS; (*6th Edition*) with additions by J. R. MARTIN, late Presidency Surgeon, and Surgeon to the Native Hospital, Calcutta. 8vo, Price 18s.

NEW MEDICAL WORKS,
PUBLISHED BY
SAMUEL HIGHLEY, 32, FLEET STREET,
OPPOSITE ST. DUNSTAN'S CHURCH.

ASHWELL ON DISEASES OF WOMEN.
Now Completed.
A PRACTICAL TREATISE ON THE DISEASES PECULIAR TO WOMEN, Comprising their Functional and Organic Affections. Illustrated by Cases derived from Hospital and Private Practice.
By SAMUEL ASHWELL, M.D., Member of the Royal College of Physicians in London, Obstetric Physician and Lecturer to Guy's Hospital, 8vo. Price £1 1s.

"In concluding our still imperfect analysis we must in justice to the author declare our conviction that his work on Female Diseases is the most able and certainly the most standard and practical we have yet seen. It will, now that it is completed, find its way into the library of every practitioner, and justly confer on its talented author, a very high place in the first class of Obstetric Physicians."—*Medico-Chirurgical Review.*

"Situated as is Dr. Ashwell in extensive practice, and at the head of the Obstetric Department of a large Hospital, it could not be but that his work must contain very valuable information—the results of great experience. The book is full of important information and excellent practical description."—*Dublin Medical Journal.*

SELECTA E PRÆSCRIPTIS; 9th Edit., Improved.
SELECTIONS FROM PHYSICIANS' PRESCRIPTIONS; containing
Lists of the Phrases, Contractions, &c., used in Prescriptions, with Explanatory Notes.
The Grammatical Constructions of Prescriptions.
Rules for the pronunciation of Pharmaceutical Terms.
A Series of (350) Abbreviated Prescriptions, illustrating the use of the preceding Terms—and
A KEY, containing the same in an Unabbreviated Form, with literal Translation.
32mo, Price 5s.

"A very useful work for Students preparing for an examination in pharmacy."—*Pharmaceutical Journal.*

A SERIES OF
ANATOMICAL SKETCHES AND DIAGRAMS.
With Descriptions and References.
BY THOMAS WORMALD and A. M. McWHINNIE,
Teachers of Practical Anatomy at St. Bartholomew's Hospital. 1 Vol. 4to. Price 26s.

"This work is now complete and is in every way calculated to fulfil its object—that of presenting a series of clear and simple Views of the more important parts of the Body—furnishing a useful guide to the Student in the Dissecting Room, and from its character as a book on Regional Anatomy, equally acceptable to the Surgeon. The subjects have been judiciously chosen, and the lithographed Drawings which are mostly coloured, are executed with great fidelity."—*Medico-Chirurgical Review.*

"Remarkable for their correctness, perspicuity, and neatness of execution."—*Forbes' Medical Review.*

THE ANATOMICAL REMEMBRANCER,
OR, COMPLETE POCKET ANATOMIST, 2nd Edition. 32mo. Price 3s. 6d.

"The Anatomy is correctly given, and the descriptions though condensed to the very highest degree, still remain clear and intelligible."—*Lancet.*

MEDICO-CHIRURGICAL REVIEW, New Series.
Arrangements have been completed to give to this Journal a development in the REVIEW DEPARTMENT, that has not been attempted by any Journal in Great Britain or elsewhere. Each Number will contain Three Hundred pages of closely printed CRITICAL ANALYSIS of all the best Works, Foreign and Domestic, forming a Quarterly LIBRARY of PROGRESSIVE PRACTICAL MEDICINE AND SURGERY.

The First Number of the New Series was published on the 1st of January, 1845.

HIGHLEY'S GENERAL MEDICAL CATALOGUE
Of Modern Works, with their Prices and Dates. Price 1s.
Corrected to the end of 1844.

Printed in Dunstable, United Kingdom